Your Mission, Should You Accept It...

An Introduction for World Christians

Stephen Gaukroger

IVP

InterVarsity Press
Downers Grove, Illinois

Foreword

Don't read this book! Stop! Right now, not another word! Well, if you must continue, just read the foreword . . . but nothing else. Okay. Good.

For a start, this book is about spreading the "good news" all over the world so everyone on the planet has a chance to know God. That is unrealistic, arrogant and unnecessary. Unrealistic because the church can't even affect the homes around it, so what hope does it have of affecting anywhere else? Arrogant because we have come to recognize, in the late twentieth century, the need to treat all religions equally and to respect the right of everyone everywhere to make up their own minds about everything, without our old-fashioned assumption that we are right. Unnecessary because through mass communication, Bible translations and the missionaries of past generations, all those who want to know about Christianity can find out without our doing anything else.

And, of course, the subject of mission is boring! Even if you do begin this book, you'll probably be asleep before you are halfway through chapter two. We have all sat through tedious presentations about God's work among the Batutsi people on the southern rim of an unpronounceable mountain range in an insignificant country with a smaller population than the Dakota Badlands. There are far more exciting things to get involved in.

People in other countries, and the unchurched all around us, don't need or want our interference in their lives. God is perfectly capable of getting their attention if he wants to. Remember this wise piece of advice:

Sit down, O men of God,

His kingdom He will bring

Whenever it may please His will;

You cannot do a thing!

The Bible itself says "charity begins at home," so let's put our energy into concerns in the church fellowship. We have plenty of problems of our own to keep us occupied. Is everything perfect in your local church? Of course not. Shouldn't we make sure that everyone is spiritually mature, emotionally happy, physically healthy, "giftedly" released and financially nonchallenged before we think about mission? Of course we should!

And in all this, remember why I was asked to write this foreword. I know more about mission than almost anyone else. You'd be amazed at the number of countries I've visited and the churches I've influenced over the years. I told Jesus to concentrate on his own needs, not to worry about the whole world. He didn't listen, and everyone knows about the sad consequences of his ignoring me—a cruel early death. I gave Paul a thorny problem to dissuade him from mission—but he went right on planting churches and evangelizing. I warned William Carey about the problems in India and Gladys Aylward about the dangers in China. I told Charles Spurgeon that there were too many orphans for his little orphanage to make any difference. I've lost count of the number of conversations I've had with Billy Graham—is anyone really listening to all those sermons? Not to mention the thousands of unknown evangelists, doctors, agriculturalists, church planters, teachers, pastors, engineers and accountants—every one a missionary—whom I've tried to persuade to leave their "ministry" and get a proper job in more comfortable surroundings. Even though I've made it clear that their churches have forgotten them and nobody remembers to pray for them, that they will probably get sick, stay poor, remain unappreciated and die misunderstood, they have refused to give up! I'm not sure what else I can do. Some people just won't take the sensible and safe option.

But I have higher hopes for the readers of this book. As we face the twenty-first century we are becoming much more sophisticated and streetwise. We know better than our predecessors and will not be fooled by a simplistic understanding of the Great Commission. When Jesus said to go into all the world and preach the good news to all creation, he obviously didn't mean what he appeared to say. Let's leave the task of world mission to the misguided, the misled and the fanatical. At last in our generation we will get this whole thing under control. You need read no further!

Lucy Fer

Chapter One

Becoming a World Christian

A world Christian isn't better than other Christians.
But by God's grace, they have made a discovery so
important that life can never be the same again.
World Christians are day-to-day disciples for whom
Christ's global cause has become the integrating,
overriding priority for all that He has for them. Like
disciples should, they actively investigate all that
their Master's great commission means. Then they
act on what they learn.
DAVID BRYANT

*E*very believer in Jesus has the incredible privilege
of sharing in his world plan. This plan excludes
no one; all people, without regard to nationality,
race, color or gender, are loved by him. He longs for
young and old, rich and poor, from the North Pole to
the South Pole, to discover this love. We are called to
be coworkers with God in putting the plan into practice
(2 Corinthians 6:1). But how? As we shall see later,
although we are called to mission, all of us are not
necessarily being called to another country, or even to

"full-time Christian service" in our own. Yet we are all called to be world Christians. Let's explore what this means, and how each of us can take practical steps to become one.

For many of us becoming a world Christian may involve a change in our *attitudes*. Sometimes we live our lives in boxes or compartments. One has the label "church" and one has the label "world." These two boxes are quite separate and distinct. "World" is bad and we should avoid contact with it as much as possible. "Church" is good and we should give time and money to it, while keeping it away from "world" so it doesn't become "worldly."

Of course there is some truth in this—the world can be a very bad place indeed. But this overall attitude can also be very dangerous, damaging our missionary impact in the world. It has led some Christians to view their lives from Monday to Saturday in a completely different way from their lives on Sunday. They see God as interested only in the *religious* parts of their lives, not in the *secular* parts such as work, home and leisure. The tragic result has been Christians with a faith that has almost no impact on their everyday lives—a faith that does not affect the way they treat their marriage partner, their colleagues at work or their relatives. Trying to keep these two boxes separate ("church" and "world") has often produced worldly Christians whose behavior is almost identical to that of the non-Christians around them. Our witness is thus neutralized in the very place it is meant to be most potent.

In addition, compartmentalization has led us to

abdicate responsibility in huge sections of modern life. A Christian ghetto claims our presence and our commitment, to the exclusion of the "bad" world which we want to avoid. Many Christians spend all their free time in church activities and meetings. They read Christian books and magazines, use their vacations to travel with other Christians to Christian conferences while listening to Christian music in the car. All their friends are Christians, and if they could they would work for a Christian company and send their children to Christian schools. It doesn't take a genius to figure out that this kind of lifestyle is going to make it a little tricky to have a significant Christian impact on our friends and neighbors.

Not that any of these things are wrong in themselves—we obviously have real needs for fellowship and teaching—but we are called to be "salty" in a bland, tasteless world and "light" in dark places (Matthew 5:13-16). We can't be these things unless we engage the non-Christian world clearly and consistently. To be a world Christian

---

Every Christian should be a World Christian, a global disciple, a Great Commission Christian, a servant of God. But what does this mean? Three commitments . . . characterise the World Christian (and should be the characteristic of every Christian).

World Christians are:

☐ Committed to God's purpose for his world.

☐ Committed to God's people who are to carry out his purpose.

☐ Committed to working out God's purpose in daily life.

Robin Thomson, World Christian *(Oxford: Lynx/St. John's Extension Studies, 1992)*

means that we do not have the luxury of opting out of contact with those who don't know Jesus.

This opting out has diminished not just our presence but also our influence in the world. Whole areas of modern life have been abandoned in favor of religious activity. Politics, economics, social action, the media, business, education, science, philosophy, the arts—all need "salty" Christians at the very highest levels. The fruit of our absence is everywhere. We complain about the influence of New Age thinking on environmentalists, for example, when instead we should be asking why Christians have been so slow to communicate the biblical position on ecological issues. Concern for creation did not begin with the green movement (see Genesis 2:15; Psalm 8; Matthew 10:29).

A world-class Christian is one whose lifestyle and obedience are compatible, in cooperation, and in accord with what God is doing and wants to do in our world.
Paul Borthwick, How to Be a World-Class Christian *(Wheaton, Ill.: Victor Books, 1993), p. 91*

World Christians have discovered that holy living is a biblical lifestyle empowered by the Spirit of their living Lord. They are not *of* this world (John 17:15-16) but are definitely *in* it. Up to their necks in it! Shining bright and being salty for Jesus.

How, in practice, can we avoid a "Christian ghetto" mindset? We can become more aware of the world and its needs by, for example,

☐ watching a news broadcast or buying a newspaper
☐ occasionally picking up a magazine that examines

world events in a thoughtful way
☐ tuning in to a documentary or panel discussion on the radio or TV rather than watching *Friends*
☐ joining a sports team or community theater group, or taking a night-school class
☐ participating in Neighborhood Watch or a residents' association
☐ subscribing to a mission magazine that reports on God's work on another continent
☐ joining the Parent-Teacher Association at the local school—or even running for the school board
☐ befriending an international student
☐ learning a foreign language
☐ visiting another country—preferably not a usual holiday destination—and staying with local people if possible

All these things will broaden our horizons and give us insights into the world of people not yet Christian—wherever in the world they may be.

But of course world Christians want to do more than understand the world; they also want to change it and support others who are trying to change it. Our actions can take a number of forms.

Communicating
World Christians are not content to talk about supporting others involved in mission—they do it! One way is to use a summer vacation to visit a Christian worker in another country. This can be wonderfully encouraging. Many missionaries have never had a visit from someone from their home church. A trip like this supports them and gives you insights you could never

get if you stayed at home

Another way is to send small gifts to a missionary. Ask to be sent their prayer letter—and read it when it comes! Perhaps you could volunteer to copy and distribute their letters to the rest of the church.

Writing letters to mission workers is a great idea. Missionaries far from home receive correspon-

How to write a good letter to a Christian worker abroad

☐ Don't be overspiritual. Feel free to write about local news items, the achievements of local sports teams or an occasional television program. Give up-to-date information on births, deaths and marriages in your church, if the missionaries are familiar with the church family. Pass on any humorous incidents too.

☐ Write on special occasions. Remember to get your card in the mail in good time for anniversaries, birthdays and Christmas. The person far from home often feels especially lonely on such occasions.

☐ Include interesting newspaper or magazine clippings, a photo of the kids or the church bulletin.

☐ Occasionally send a postcard, perhaps when you are on vacation. It will be encouraging for your missionary friends to receive invitations to weddings too. Even if they will not be able to come, they will feel less left out.

☐ Say you are praying for them (and do it!). Offer a verse from the Bible to encourage them.

☐ Do not expect a reply to every letter.

☐ Experiment with putting a message on cassette or making an annual phone call.

☐ Be creative! Try to put yourself in their position and respond accordingly.

dence with an enthusiasm far in excess of the energy it takes to write it. You may even be able to fax or e-mail your letter, depending on the resources available to the missionary.

When missionaries return for a home visit, take them out for a meal or to see a play. Plan to be at least as supportive when they come home as you are when they are away.

Praying

What we pray about reveals our priorities (such as health, money, family, good weather). It works in reverse too—we can pray about mission until it *becomes* a priority! We may not personally be able to take the good news abroad, but all of us can affect the world through prayer. Individuals, and whole churches, need to rediscover the power of prayer and the sheer thrill of participating in God's purposes by praying.

Prayer requires no passport, visa or work permit. There is no such thing as a "closed country" as far as prayer is concerned. It doesn't suffer from jet lag, language problems or cultural adjustment. It can cross thousands of miles and any number of time zones, penetrate any building, in any weather . . . and all in less than a split second! Prayer is God's strategy for making plain the defeat of his enemies.

Much of the history of mission could be written in terms of God's moving in response to persistent prayer. In fact, mission history is filled with stories of how Christians felt compelled to pray at precisely the time when a missionary was facing a crisis—completely unknown to the person who was driven to prayer.

Disaster has been averted, death prevented, break-throughs in evangelism seen—all in response to prayer. And, no less important, the routine, day-to-day work of mission is sustained through regular, faithful pray-ing. Despite overwhelming opposition, prayer sees God's work continue undefeated. In some parts of the world it is almost impossible to explain the continued presence of Christian missionaries without acknowl-edging the role of prayer.

Leaders in mission are often the quickest to admit their need of prayer and are the greatest believers in its power. Hudson Taylor, for example, was instrumen-tal in seeing God's love released in China. First he prayed for seventy mission workers in a year, then a hundred the next, and then a thousand new workers over five years. God answered all these requests: the

The need for praying people

I am persuaded that England is rich in godly, quiet, praying people, in every denomination. They may not be a great multitude as far as numbers are concerned, but they are "rich in faith," even if many of them be poor and of humble station. It is the prayers of such that I covet more than the gold of Ophir—those good old men and good old women (yes, and not necessarily old either) who know what it is to have power with God and prevail. . . . Will you help me, prayerfully and judiciously, to get some of these to join the circle? . . . The work for which I am asking prayer is the preaching and teaching [of] the Word of God, pure and simple. . . . I have no confidence in anything but the Gospel of Calvary to uplift these needy people.

Letter of James Frazer, missionary to the Lisu people, China; quoted in Eileen Crossman, Mountain Rain *(Littleton, Colo.: OMF, 1988)*

China Inland Mission was born, and this huge nation was exposed to the gospel.

> The church has many organizers, but few agonizers; many who pay, but few who pray; many resters, but few wrestlers; many who are enterprising, but few who are interceding. The secret of praying is praying in secret. That is the difference between the modern church and the early church. In the matter of effective praying, never have so many left so much to so few. Let us pray!
> *Leonard Ravenhill*

We can all pray privately for some aspect of mission. Our prayer should be informed, persistent and expectant. We could join a missionary prayer group or form a prayer partnership with world mission as a focus. We could set aside an hour a week to pray specifically for mission.

Being a world Christian

"It's all right for you to advocate all Christians should be global Christians. You've traveled constantly and from what you've said, you certainly adapt extremely well to new friends and cultures. My world is rather different. I spend more time with animals than with human beings. My wife and I had to summon up extra reserves of courage just to cross the channel for a day trip to France." Mr. Lester was a dairy farmer from Yorkshire and he rarely minced his words. He was visiting his daughter in Southampton and heard me speaking at a missionary weekend. Before I could comment he went on, "Moreover, your job and your organization force you to be a world Christian. What about ordinary believers like myself?"

I asked him whether he watched the news on TV. "Of course I do—every day. I carry a small transistor radio with me and I tune to the BBC World Service." "That's excellent," I retorted. "That's where I get most of my material for global praying." He looked rather surprised. I explained that national and world news always provided me with splendid opportunities for intercession. At that time the famine in Ethiopia and Sudan was grabbing the headlines. The tragic scenes of poverty, death and misery triggered me to pray for the leaders of both nations, as well as the victims of malnutrition and famine. I showed Mr. Lester *Operation World* by Patrick Johnstone. I explained, "This is an excellent resource book for global Christians. It's packed with concise information on every nation. When a news item strikes me, I consult this book to find out more about the country that's making the news."

We decided to check out Ethiopia and Sudan. Within minutes we gleaned vital information on both countries. We studied the population figures and compared the relative strength of the church in both countries. We immediately discerned that the Christians in southern Sudan were in the majority, but in the north they were in a minority under the Arabs.

We read useful statistics about the size and influence of the Ethiopian Orthodox Church and its hostility towards Protestants. The prayer requests enabled us to target specific prayers for both nations. By then Mr. Lester was getting rather excited. "Hey, this is thrilling! I can be a world Christian where I am; my papers and TV news broadcasts can serve as prompts for prayer. Thank you for introducing me to *Operation World*—where can I buy a copy?" Thankfully, he was able to purchase a copy from the church book table.

Chua Wee Hian, Getting Through Customs *(Leicester, England: Inter-Varsity Press, 1992), pp. 180-81*

Some Christians plan to fast on one day each month and use the time they would spend on eating in prayer for world concerns. Whatever we do, we must pray.

Giving

God's work needs God's money to be released through God's people. Not all the churches in New Testament times had grasped this, and Paul himself seems to have been adequately supported only by the Christians in Philippi (Philippians 4:14-18). The church at Corinth needed a reminder to be generous (2 Corinthians 9:1), and Timothy was challenged about the dangers of materialism (1 Timothy 6:6-10). How we need to hear this again today.

Much mission work today is in financial crisis. Mission agencies have found themselves letting staff go, freezing salaries and restricting the development of new projects. Literature remains unprinted, or if printed, it goes undistributed. Money for facilities and equipment isn't available, so organizations struggle with inadequate buildings, outdated computers and photocopiers, and unreliable vehicles. This makes an organization expensive to run and relatively inefficient. Yet the resources are available if only God's people would release them.

A biblical lifestyle demands generous giving. Perhaps every Christian should have a "giving goal" toward which they aim. This could be something like "to give 10 percent of my income to the local church and 5 percent of my income to world mission by five years from now." No Christian can tell another how much to give, so we must never feel bullied or pressured. Personal circumstances such as debt, children, employment and savings vary enormously, but every believer has a responsibility before God to give sacrificially.

It is important to set aside your missions money as soon as you receive it—every week or every month—rather than waiting to see what is left after you pay other bills. Some people find it helpful to put cash into a simple collecting box on the same day each week or month. Others write regular checks or sign up for automatic withdrawals from their bank account.

Thinking

World Christians engage their brains in trying to understand the complexities of today's international community. (This challenge is more appealing to some of us than others!) World mission currently faces some difficult questions: What right do we have to interfere with another country's culture, religion and heritage? Don't missionaries create more problems than they

Anthropologists identify the earliest stages of societies as "hunters and gatherers," those people who have foraged through the fields and forests gathering berries and roots and other edibles for their sustenance. I like to think of world-class Christians as "hunters and gatherers" in a different way. To further our growth, we are always hunting for information and gathering data about issues in the world into which God calls us. We continue to grow by foraging through books, newspapers, and a host of other sources to expand our minds concerning God's great world.
Paul Borthwick, How to Be a World-Class Christian *(Wheaton, Ill.: Victor Books, 1993), p. 24*

solve (adding to political instability, creating unmet wants and unnecessary dissatisfaction with the status quo)? Why do we need to send missionaries to parts of the world where the church is growing faster than it is here at home? Some Christians have been so embarrassed by these questions that they have let mission slip off the agenda.

But if we want our Christian faith to be thoughtful and consistent, we will meet such questions head-on. The good news is that while these questions may be new to us, most of the best mission agencies have been grappling with them for a long time. In fact, criticism of foreign missionaries goes back a long way. Almost two hundred years ago, at the start of the nineteenth century, representatives of the British East India Company said, "The sending of Christian Missionaries into our eastern possessions is the maddest, most expensive, most unwarranted project that was ever proposed by a lunatic enthusiast!" However, by the close of the nineteenth century, a hundred years later, the governor of Bengal was saying, "In my judgment, Christian missionaries have done more lasting good to the people of India than all the other agencies combined."

It is worth asking these same "difficult" questions about Islamic or Hindu missions and missionaries. Do you think posing such questions will slow the building of mosques in non-Islamic countries? (All those who answer yes to this question—I have some land on Jupiter to sell you!) Why don't other countries give the same freedom to Christianity that the United States, for example, gives to their predominant religion? And perhaps we send missionaries to Brazil and Korea (where church growth is rapid) because the churches in these countries still ask us to! Often where there are thousands of new converts there is a huge need for leadership training, advice on pastoral care and teaching in discipleship. What we learn in these situations we can bring back home to reinvigorate the Western church. And we do have a great deal to learn from the rest of the world. Almost three-quarters of all evangelical Christians now live in the Two-Thirds World. Britain, for instance, may soon be receiving more missionaries than it sends abroad. World mission gives us a great opportunity to get involved in what God is doing on every continent—receiving just as much as we contribute to others.

So the next time you encounter a cynical TV documentary or newspaper article about missionaries—don't worry! It might help to write down the questions that trouble you and send them to a mission agency, asking for their response. Alternatively, ask the manager of your local Christian bookstore for some material, or talk to your minister or to a missionary on home assignment. There are good, satisfying answers to these questions!

Study Guide
Read John 4:27-38.

1. "A world Christian is someone who . . ." Using this chapter, draw up a definition of a world Christian. Do this as a group, or in threes, then share your definitions to come up with a composite.

2. On pages 17-24 we read of praying, giving and thinking as a world Christian. Which of these is your strongest area, and which is your weakest? How can you develop your strength and strengthen your weakness?

3. Compare notes to discover the strengths and weaknesses of your group as a whole.

4. Consider the key passage above. Why do you think the disciples failed to "see the harvest field"?

How might Jesus' comments on sowers and reapers apply to being a world Christian?

Chapter Two

The Ultimate Authority

*T*he Bible says a lot of things, but "charity begins at home" isn't one of them. If we have any authority at all to take the gospel to our neighbors and the world, we will have to find it in the Bible. We are people under authority. We don't have the luxury of "making it up as we go along." What we believe and how we act in areas such as sexuality, spiritual gifts and worship should flow out of an understanding of what the Bible says. This applies to mission as well. If the Bible says nothing about it, let's stay at home, put our feet up and channel-surf with the remote control!

On the other hand, if our Handbook does have something to say on the subject, we should find out what it is and then get on with doing what it says. Well, it does, and we should!

Mission in the Old Testament

From the very beginning God demonstrates a commitment to help people get to know him and live together in peace and joy. Adam and Eve reject God's plan and have to face the consequence—separation from God and some hostility in their relationship with each other. God doesn't give up on them, or their family. He still wants a relationship with them, even though they have turned their backs on him.

This scenario has been repeated millions of times in human history—and God's response has been consistent. His character of total goodness can't stand evil, but he goes on loving those who do evil, always wanting them to come back to him. His "mission statement" has always included taking deliberate steps to go and look for people who are hiding from him, or who are looking for him but have gotten lost. In the Garden of Eden he gets involved in the world's first-ever game of hide-and-seek (Genesis 3:8-19). Adam and Eve are found, then found out (vv. 11-13), then thrown out (v. 23). But God doesn't give up on them or their dependents; he is always looking for ways to draw them back into conversation and relationship. You can see this in the stories of Cain (4:13-15), Enoch (5:24) and Noah (6:8).

And although it is soon obvious that a specific nation, the Jews, has been chosen as a channel of God's message, they are not to be the only ones who benefit. Throughout the Old Testament, Gentiles and Jews—the whole world in fact—are the focus of God's search-and-rescue mission.

> All the ends of the earth
>> will remember and turn to the Lord,

and all the families of the nations
    will bow down before him. (Psalm 22:27)
In Isaiah 49:6 the Lord says,
    It is too small a thing for you to be my servant
        to restore the tribes of Jacob
        and bring those of Israel I have kept.
    I will also make you a light for the Gentiles,
        that you may bring my salvation to the ends of the
          earth.
It's pretty clear that our God wants everyone in every nation to be part of his family!

> "My name will be great among the nations, from the rising to the setting of the sun. In every place incense and pure offerings will be brought to my name, because my name will be great among the nations," says the LORD Almighty.
> *Malachi 1:11*

Mission in the New Testament
This missionary emphasis in the Godhead continued in the arrival of God's Son (whose mission statement was "For the Son of Man came to seek and to save what was lost"—Luke 19:10). His whole life, the death he died and the miracle of his resurrection—all were directed at pleasing his mission-minded Father (John 8:28-29).

    God's will is that this mission-task be passed on to the church. God sent his Son, and his Son sends us. When Jesus declared, "Peace be with you! As the Father has sent me, I am sending you" (John 20:21), he makes this remarkable idea clear. We have the

These early Christians [in the book of Acts] were led by the Spirit to the main task of bringing people to God through Christ, and were not permitted to enjoy fascinating sidetracks.
J. B. Phillips

There is no argument for missions. The total action of God in history, the whole revelation of God in Christ— this is the argument.
James S. Stewart

The Spirit of Christ is the spirit of missions, and the nearer we get to him the more intensely missionary we must become.
Henry Martyn

The Bible is a missionary book. Jesus Christ is the Father's missionary to a lost world.
Harold Lindsell

incredible privilege of sharing with the Father and the Son the job of going to the world with the good news. David Livingstone summed it up when he said, "God had an only Son, and he was a missionary and a physician. A poor, poor imitation of Him I am, or wish to be."

And it seems that the early church got the message. From Pentecost onward they saw their primary task as living in a new way and explaining this "way" to all who would listen. Three thousand responded on the day of Pentecost (Acts 2:41), another five thousand within a few weeks (Acts 4:4); and from then on there is a constant series of references to people responding to their missionary outreach (Acts 2:45; 5:14; 6:7 and so on).

And the growth was not simply numerical. The missionary zeal of the early church pushed back the boundaries of gender, color, race and nationality. This message was for everyone, this mission universal (Acts 1:8). In a thrilling series of raids on enemy territory, the gospel penetrated far beyond its early male, Jewish origins. The hated Samaritans (Acts 8:5), a black African (8:26-39), a religious bigot (9:1-19), a woman (9:36) and a Roman centurion (10:1)—do these Christians have no discernment? They seem willing to take the gospel to anyone! Just like Jesus, the early church is led into feeding the hungry, looking after the poor and healing the sick. This mission, his mission, was their constant preoccupation. Acts 5:42 seems a pretty clear description of the working out of their own mission statement: "Day after day, in the temple courts and from house to house, they never stopped teaching and proclaiming the good news that Jesus is the Christ."

The two leading characters of the New Testament church demonstrate this mission enthusiasm in both their lives and their letters: Peter, senior apostle and local evangelist, and Paul, globetrotting missionary statesman. Peter is captivated by a God who longs for everyone to know him (2 Peter 3:9)—even the Romans who have conquered the Jews and now rule over them (see Acts 10:1), unclean Gentiles (Acts 11:1-3)! Paul is converted and commissioned in an unmistakable encounter with Jesus in the suburbs of Damascus (Acts 9:15). And after years of church planting and evangelistic preaching, he still can't get over the wonder of a God who wants all of humanity, without distinction, to share this marvelous good news (Ephesians 3:6).

If a man goes overseas for any length of time we would expect him to learn the language of the country to which he is going. More than this is needed, however, if he is really to communicate with the people among whom he is living. He must learn another language—that of the thought-forms of the people to whom he speaks. Only so will he have real communication with them and to them. So it is with the Christian church. Its responsibility is not only to hold to the basic, scriptural principles of the Christian faith, but to communicate these unchanging truths "into" the generation in which it is living.

Every generation of Christians has this problem of learning how to speak meaningfully to its own age. . . . If we are to communicate the Christian faith effectively, therefore, we must know and understand the thought-forms of our own generation. These will differ slightly from place to place, and more so from nation to nation.

Francis Schaeffer, Escape from Reason *(Downers Grove, Ill.: Inter-Varsity Press, 1968)*

So far we have discovered that God is mission-oriented by nature and activity. So was his Son, and so was the early church. The Bible is shot through with this missionary spirit. But is it merely a *description* of the way things were, or is it a *prescription* for the way things ought to be? What does the Bible have to say about the role of individual Christians and of the church as a whole today? The Bible affirms three principles that are vitally important: a *continuing* mission, a *command* to mission and a *climax* to mission.

A Continuing Mission

Jesus is pretty clear that the missionary task will not end when he dies; in fact, his death and resurrection will signal its beginning (John 20:19-23). The drawing of people to him was obviously going to take some time. Jesus anticipated that there would be believers he would never meet in the flesh; as evangelism continued, converts would go on multiplying as his disciples made other disciples, and so on: "My prayer is not for them alone. I pray also for those who will believe in me through their message" (John 17:20).

Jesus assumed that some time would elapse between his death and resurrection and his Second Coming. The period between his two appearances on our planet was to be taken up with missionary activity. When the whole world had heard, this would be the cue for his return to the world stage (Matthew 24:14). Christians entering the twenty-first century are part of this "between appearances" mission team.

A Command to Mission
One of Jesus' last instructions to his followers had to do with the missionary task. Mark and Luke summarize this command (Mark 16:15; Luke 24:47-48), but perhaps the fullest account is in Matthew's Gospel (Matthew 28:18-20). "Make disciples," commands Jesus. "As you go about your business, wherever you travel in the nations of the world, baptize and teach." Jesus is at pains to point out that this discipling responsibility will continue to the "end of the age," so he promises that his presence will continue with his people until the missionary task is completed. His command is to be fulfilled in the light of this comfort: "I will be with you always."

So the command (and the comfort) is not time-limited. This is not a specific command to a particular group of first-century Jewish men. It is a command to disciples of Jesus in every age, to be obeyed until the final age dawns. The church has its marching orders from the commander-in-chief. Our role as individual believers may vary depending on our gifts and calling, but no disciple of Jesus can evade the thrust of his command. Only the King's return will remove the obligation of obeying the King's command.

And this command is just as relevant in our world of many religions as it has ever been. We must obey the command sensitively, with tact and great respect for the followers of other religions. But we can't evade the truth that Jesus claimed: "I am the way and the truth and the life. No one comes to the Father except through me" (John 14:6). The command to evangelize is based on this fact.

The Climax of Mission

The Bible has a captivating view of the goal or climax of mission. It describes a future in which every language, people-group and country will be represented in a magnificent display of international cooperation and harmony (Revelation 7:9). The whole of history is moving toward this stupendous conclusion: a planetwide worship and celebration event with participants from all the nations of the globe under the lordship of Jesus.

This event draws us into its fulfillment. As believers, we will be present. We are invited to participate in the destiny that God has prepared for all who love him. And mission is the privilege we have of inviting others to share in this glorious future.

Sadly, the Bible also speaks of an alternative climax or destiny for the human race. Just as there is a heaven to be enjoyed, so there is a hell to be avoided. The Bible's teaching on judgment seems very harsh in these enlightened and tolerant times. But it is hard to get away from the fact that permanent separation from God will be the consequence of rejecting him (Matthew 25:41, 46; Mark 9:43-44; John 3:36).

All your life an unattainable ecstasy has hovered just beyond the grasp of your consciousness. The day is coming when you will wake to find, beyond all hope, that you have attained it, or else, that it was within your reach and you have lost it forever.
C. S. Lewis, "Heaven," in The Problem of Pain (London: Geoffrey Bles, 1945), p. 136

A strong motivation for mission is found in the Bible's teaching about the fate of those who refuse God's offer of love. Much of our personal evangelism and local church commitment to mission will be halfhearted until the awfulness of the destiny of the lost hits us. Too many of us are "closet universalists"—surely it will all work out for everyone in the end, we reason. Unfortunately, the Bible offers us no such assurance.

The Bible offers two destinies to the people of planet Earth. Mission is the church's way of encouraging participation in the heavenly destiny and showing how the hellish destiny can be avoided. Either way, our destiny as believers compels us to invite other people to consider their own.

How can a God of love send people to hell?

Hell means total separation from everything good. The flames described in the Bible may be picture language, but the reality they represent is no figment of the imagination. One of the reasons it exists is because of the seriousness with which God takes the decisions of men and women. If we choose to reject him and his offer of life, with his way of escape from all the dirtiness in the world, he refuses to overrule our decision. He won't force us to accept his love, because that would rob us of the privilege of choice and make us mere robots. So we do have to take the consequences of our decisions. Which means by choosing to live without God we have indeed chosen to live without God—now and forever. And it is no use asking why we can't choose to live without God in this life, but choose to live with him in the next. The question completely misses the point about the radical nature of the choice. It's as if we wanted to choose not to have any children of our own and then at the age of eighty to change our mind and want to have grown-up children around to look after us. It's too late; our earlier decision has had inevitable consequences. So it is with our decision about God. There comes a point (death) when our earlier decision is too far gone to change. Which means we have chosen to spend eternity living in the presence of our own sinfulness and in the absence of God.

All of this means that, far from God sending us to hell, we seem to be sending ourselves. After all, it would be most unreasonable to blame the doctor for our ill health if we refuse to take the medicine he prescribed! The divine doctor has diagnosed the sinsickness of mankind and offered a forgiveness-cure. If we refuse or ignore the offer we will have to live with the disease. And that's what hell is: living after death with all our worst traits still raging inside us. But now they are unrestrained by God or social convention—a seething mass

of unforgiven vices and unresolved conflicts. God does not want anyone to go to hell and so he has prepared a way for mankind to escape its horrors. He is in the business of getting people into heaven and not sending them to hell.
Stephen Gaukroger, It Makes Sense *(London: Scripture Union, 1987)*

So the Bible points us to the priority of mission with a relentless logic and a passionate enthusiasm. The nature and activity of God the Father, the work and words of God's Son and the example of the early church empowered by the Holy Spirit are clear. The Holy Spirit goes on applying the Scripture to our lives as we bring ourselves under its authority. We are commanded to be activists in the cause of mission, right up to the return of Jesus, preparing for the great destiny that awaits us.

Fundamentally, the Bible affirms that our Christian faith is a mission-faith. If it isn't, we ought to question whether it is biblical faith at all.

Study Guide
Read Matthew 25:41-46; 28:18-20; John 17:20. Then review the sections in this chapter called "A Continuing Mission," "A Command to Mission" and "The Climax of Mission."

1. How do you suppose the eleven disciples felt on hearing the Great Commission, Jesus' words in Matthew 28:18-20?

2. How do *you* feel about being part of Jesus' "between appearances" mission team?

3. What do you think motivated the disciples to be obedient to the command?

4. What motivates you?

5. What things hinder you from full involvement in the team, and how can these hindrances be overcome?

6. In what ways are you currently involved in making other disciples?

7. How can you encourage one another in your group to be active members of this mission team?

Chapter Three

What Is a Missionary?

*I*s it a bird? Is it a plane? No! It's a missionary! For quite a large number of Christians even the word *missionary* is a turnoff; no wonder so few ever think about becoming one. *Missionary.* Images from a colonial past may flash before our eyes: tea on a wooden veranda, with a black houseboy standing by; pith helmets, khaki shorts and natives with bundles on their heads. Or perhaps we think of street-corner evangelists bellowing King James English to bemused passersby. Isn't there something slightly eccentric about a "missionary"?

Such dreadful caricatures are sometimes confirmed when you meet missionaries on leave in the West. They can appear out of touch in dress, style of presentation and attitude, reinforcing the impression that missionaries (and so mission) are out of date and out of touch.

None of this exactly serves to get you rushing to see your minister and offer your services in mission—here or overseas. It would be bad for your image; there are other more attractive things to be getting involved with.

Despite all this, mission is incredibly important: it's a vital, biblical focus of the church of Jesus. And to do mission we obviously need people to do it—"missionaries," or God's mission agents. Thousands of them, young and old, employed and unemployed, single and married, a whole army for God's kingdom purposes in the world.

I suppose changing the name might help, but to what? Gospel-truth transmitter? Aide to the spiritually challenged? There don't seem to be too many obvious alternatives. The use of "international partner" is a recent attempt to emphasize that mission work today is often with and under the authority of national leadership.

But until we come up with a more acceptable name, it may be best to focus on getting a handle on what missionaries or mission-motivated Christians actually do. What is this "mission" they are engaged in?

Mission involves "all that God sent his people in the world to do," to quote John Stott. This includes telling people about God in a way they can understand. It includes wanting people to have access to a local worshiping community and at least some of the Bible in their own language. It includes wanting hunger to be alleviated and disease to be minimized. It includes wanting freedom from torture, oppression and war. It includes wanting to make disciples of Jesus Christ. It includes wanting the whole world to receive the benefits of being part of the kingdom of God. It includes wanting God's will to be done on earth, as it is in heaven. This is mission.

The Crosscultural Missionary

Definition: one who is commissioned and sent out by a local church to cross cultural boundaries in order to be a witness for Jesus Christ. These boundaries may be those of language, geography or society.

The crosscultural missionary would also intentionally

☐ introduce people to Christ by his or her life, attitudes, actions and words

☐ help those who come to Christ to join with others in the fellowship of a church (a church will need to be planted, if it doesn't exist!)

In Ephesians 4:11-16 Paul clearly shows that our ascended Lord gave gifts of different kinds to people for different tasks within his kingdom. Not every Christian is a pastor or an apostle, an evangelist or a teacher. Similarly, we are not all called to be crosscultural missionaries in the sense described above. But we all are called to be involved in God's mission in one way or another. Some of us will cross the boundaries of society, geography and language. Others of us will provide support through our love, prayers, gifts and commitment.

To take an analogy from the army, all Christians are under the command of Christ. We recognize that he is the supreme commander. We are committed to his purposes of reconciling everything to himself—things on earth and in heaven (Colossians 1:19-20). But some of us are commanded to be frontline personnel, going to places where the claims of Jesus are not yet recognized. In military terms, these could be the infantry, paratroopers and marines. These frontliners would be backed up by the artillery, engineers, transport and support personnel. The frontline troops, however, also need the backup of logistics specialists, with their expertise in catering, administration, intelligence and a host of other things, to maintain the frontline operation over long periods of time.

The enterprise of crosscultural mission needs the resources and commitment of the whole body of the church, both in "sending" and in "receiving" countries. The crosscultural missionary relies on this web of support and cannot function without it.

This sounds much more exciting than "being a missionary," but it simply describes what true missionaries have always been about. They may have been working in Boston or Buenos Aires, pastoring or planting crops, a mile or five thousand miles from home.

Everyone involved in God's mission is a witness. And this witness can be described in three different but complementary ways. It is about *encountering, telling* and *demonstrating*. Any one of these may be our primary personal calling as an agent of mission, but the mission task of the church involves all three elements.

Encountering

The mission of Jesus was a mission where things happened! And some of these things were not your run-of-the-mill events. Blind eyes started seeing (John

9:25), leprosy patients got cured (Luke 17:11-14) and even dead people came back to life (John 11:43-44). What's more, those whose lives had been invaded by evil—messing them up emotionally, mentally and spiritually—found Satan being unceremoniously kicked out (Luke 8:27-33).

The early church continued this tradition of seeing God move in power. Disabled beggars leaped to their feet (Acts 3:6-8), there was a miraculous jailbreak (Acts 12:5-10), and the devil-inspired opposition was effectively silenced (Acts 13:9-11)!

The mission of the church involves a clash of two kingdoms—God's and Satan's. Our mission is to mount raids on Satan's kingdom, setting free his captives. This is warfare, and our weapons are not forged by human ingenuity but by spiritual power. That is, mission is a supernatural activity. The world, the flesh and the devil do not yield territory without a fight. A living encounter with Jesus is what serves these enemies of God with their eviction notice.

Behind many social ills lie dark spiritual forces; demonic agencies may be at work behind political and social institutions that hinder the spread of the gospel. The point of this statement is not to make us paranoid so that we imagine the devil croppping up everywhere, but to remind us that he has already been disarmed (Colossians 2:15) and we should see that he is fully routed and put into retreat.

Mission that lacks this dimension of encounter is not fully biblical. Many advances for the gospel in both "telling" and "demonstrating" have occurred when there has been clear evidence of God at work. Through-

The tax collector in Torgau and the counselor in Belgern have written to me to ask that I offer some good advice and help for Mrs. John Korner's afflicted husband. I know of no worldly help to give. If the physicians are at a loss to find a remedy, you may be sure that it is not a case of ordinary melancholy. It must, rather, be an affliction that comes from the devil, and this must be counteracted by the power of Christ with the prayer of faith. This is what we do, and what we have been accustomed to do, for a cabinet maker here was similarly afflicted with madness and we cured him by prayer in Christ's name.

Accordingly you should proceed as follows: Go to him with a deacon and two or three good men. Confident that you, as pastor of the place, are clothed with the authority of the ministerial office, lay your hands upon him and say, "Peace be with you, dear brother, from God our Father and from our Lord Jesus Christ." Thereupon repeat the Creed and the Lord's Prayer over him in a clear voice, and close with these words: "O God, almighty Father, who has told us through thy Son, 'Verily, verily I say unto you, Whatsoever ye shall ask the Father in my name, he will give it to you'; who has commanded and encouraged us to pray in his name, 'Ask, and ye shall receive,' and who in like manner has said, 'Call upon me in the day of trouble: I will deliver thee, and thou shalt glorify me'; we unworthy sinners, relying on these thy words and commands, pray for thy mercy with such faith as we can muster. Graciously deign to free this man from all evil, and put to nought the work that Satan has done in him, to the honor of thy name and the strengthening of the faith of believers; through the same Jesus Christ, thy Son, our Lord, who liveth and reigneth with thee, world without end. Amen." Then, when you depart, lay your hands upon the man again and say, "These signs shall follow them that believe; they shall lay hands on the sick, and they shall recover."

Martin Luther

out church history there has been an awareness of God's power in mission, especially through healing and deliverance from demons.

Mission workers in many parts of the world today tell of an oppressive atmosphere and clear evidence of the devil's control of people's lives. I recently spoke with someone who had just returned from a remote part of north India. This person had come across children deliberately mutilated to aid in begging, baby girls murdered to avoid the expense of raising them, and an all-pervading, almost intangible sense of evil. In such an environment, spiritual authority is not a subject to be discussed but a power to be exercised for the sake of survival.

In the West too we are constantly reminded of the presence and activity of evil, in publicity like that surrounding the murder of Nicole Brown Simpson, the trial of an English husband and wife for the murder of many young people, including their own daughter, and allegations of sordid sexual abuse.

Telling

People everywhere need to hear the good news explained to them in ways they can understand. Romans 10:13-14 highlights the importance of this: " 'Everyone who calls on the name of the Lord will be saved.' How, then, can they call on the one they have not believed in? And how can they believe in the one of whom they have not heard? And how can they hear without someone preaching to them?"

There is simply no substitute for preaching the truth—whether to individuals or to a huge crowd—explaining the basic facts of the gospel and calling for a response. Of course this must be done sensitively, humbly and in a way that is culturally appropriate. We will want to take great care to avoid unnecessary offense by our tone, dress, use of illustrations and style of presentation. Whether we are preaching in a pub in England or a marketplace in India, we will always want to treat our hearers with respect. We will plan to avoid manipulative techniques and tricks or gimmicks that would trivialize our message.

Certainly we must act in these wise ways—but we must still act! Sometimes we become so sophisticated, so "careful," that the simple power of the gospel is all but extinguished. The roar of the Lion of Judah has become the muted *meow* of a castrated tomcat!

The good news desperately needs telling. Millions are going to an eternity without God. Who will tell them of God's amazing love for them, his longing to see them set free from wrong, filled with his love and power, guaranteed a relationship with him forever? How can they find out about all this if no one tells them?

Sometimes telling is the hardest and most easily forgotten part of mission. Lots of countries that accept Christian doctors or agriculturalists deny access to evangelists and pastors. This means that "telling" has to be done discreetly and cautiously; there is often great pressure on missionaries not to tell at all. Even in the West we know what a struggle it is to get beyond friendship evangelism to articulating the gospel. Some of us have had non-Christian friends, family or neighbors for years, and they have never heard us describe our Christian faith. We had hoped our Christian lifestyle would prompt them to ask questions, but they seem remarkably uncurious! And of course we don't want to be pushy and embarrass them, or us, so we say nothing. Sometimes our silence is actually yellow rather than golden!

Mission involves verbal communication. We have a message to pass on to the world—a message that people need to hear, understand and respond to. This message involves concepts such as repentance, faith and forgiveness. Its statements of truth demand a response. The words of an African inquirer in the first century sum up the cry of a needy world today:

> The Spirit told Philip, "Go to that chariot and stay near it."
>
> Then Philip ran up to the chariot and heard the man reading Isaiah the prophet. "Do you understand what you are reading?" Philip asked.
>
> "How can I," he said, "unless someone explains it to me?" So he invited Philip to come up and sit with him. (Acts 8:29-31)

Philip told the African leader about Jesus, and he responded with faith, asking for baptism. Telling helped this individual to move from inquiring to deciding.

Demonstrating

The Bible consistently describes mission in terms of compassion as well as communication—that is, works as well as words. The Old Testament encouraged acts of kindness, particularly to the poor, famished and homeless (Isaiah 58:7). Jesus spent a lot of time meeting people's physical needs: healing the sick (as in Luke

8:48), feeding the hungry (as in Luke 9:16-17), even rescuing frightened fishermen on a stormy lake (Mark 4:38-39).

Jesus also made it clear that these practical demonstrations of God's love were to be continued by the church (Matthew 25:31-46), not as an optional extra but as an integral part of the missionary task. "Demonstrations" of the good news are not more inferior expressions of mission than "telling," nor are they replacements for "telling"—they are partners in the mission!

The need for these practical acts of care is obvious everywhere in our hurting world. Our television screens and newspapers bombard us with images of famine, earthquake and flood. In the towns and cities of our own Western countries, the homeless sleep in gutters, debt cripples thousands of families, and children are abused and neglected. Jesus hears the cry of the hurting, and our mission is to respond in love. These are people for whom Christ died, people Jesus loves. He wants to use the church to answer their anguished prayers for help. They can't eat a portion of Scripture or live in a sermon! Compassion demands a different response.

Good deeds that demonstrate God's love often open up opportunities for telling that otherwise would have fallen on deaf ears. Christian action can prepare the way for Christian preaching. But we must be careful not to be manipulative. These "demonstrations" are to be done because they are part of mission, part of acting on the way God feels about our broken world, not simply as means to make people more responsive to evangelism.

Jesus was not afraid to look human need in the face, in all its ugly reality. And what he saw invariably moved him to compassion, and so to compassionate service. Sometimes, he spoke. But his compassion never dissipated itself in words; it found expression in deeds. He saw, he felt, he acted. The movement was from the eye to the heart, and from the heart to the hand. His compassion was always aroused by the sight of need, and it always led to constructive action.

It seems incontrovertible that if we are even to begin to follow the real Jesus, and to walk in his shoes, we must seize every opportunity to "do good." Our good works will show the genuineness of our love, and our love will show the genuineness of our faith.
John R. W. Stott

Many non-Christians in the past have "converted" as a way of keeping the church's practical support coming! Their faith lasts as long as the money continues. We must not encourage this kind of response by attaching strings to our care for the needy. The hungry must be fed, whether or not they turn to Christ. Of course we long for them to know him, but care is an action that needs no "spiritual" justification.

So being a partner in mission means being part of God's mission to his world. This mission, for which the whole church bears responsibility, involves *encountering, telling* and *demonstrating* the gospel. Only this *whole* gospel has a hope of reaching the whole world.

Study Guide

Read John 17:11-23; Romans 10:13-14.

1. "Everyone involved in God's mission is a witness. And this witness can be described in three different but complementary ways. It is about *encountering, telling* and *demon-strating*" (p. 42). In which of these three areas do you personally have the most experience?

2. Are there any in which you have no experience? What first steps can you make in that area?

3. Most Western Christians have fears when it comes to speaking to others about Christ. What specifically are we afraid of? What Scriptures can you bring to bear on these fears?

4. What one step will you take this week to face one of your fears and overcome it? How can the group support you in this?

5. Which do you think is easier and why: to tell the gospel message to people in your own country or to go to another culture to tell it?

Chapter Four

Who Will Go?

"Woe to me!" I cried. "I am ruined! For I am a man of unclean lips, and I live among a people of unclean lips, and my eyes have seen the King, the LORD Almighty."

Then one of the seraphs flew to me with a live coal in his hand, which he had taken with tongs from the altar. With it he touched my mouth and said, "See, this has touched your lips; your guilt is taken away and your sin atoned for."

Then I heard the voice of the Lord saying, "Whom shall I send? And who will go for us?"

And I said, "Here am I. Send me!"

ISAIAH 6:5-8

God's mission needs people who will go. Men and women who have heard his call and respond with obedience. Not superheroes who leap over all obstacles with a single bound. Not megasaints who have never had an ungodly thought in their lives. Not spiritual giants who have already memorized the entire Old Testament. God's mission needs ordinary men and women who want to do what God wants them to do, above everything else. This means you or me, or the person in the seat next to me in church.

Years ago Admiral Foote was visiting Siam (now Thailand) and had invited the king and members of the royal court to a dinner on his ship. Before the meal was served he prayed, asking God to bless the food. When he had finished, the king of Siam said that he thought only missionaries prayed before eating a meal. The admiral replied cheerfully, "Yes, but every Christian is a missionary!"

Every Christian is called to be a missionary in the sense that we are witnesses to what God has done in our lives, and wherever we go we must be his messengers through holy lives and spoken witness. Not all are called to dedicate their life to "full-time Christian service" either here or overseas. But many are called to be God's mission agents in banking, education, medicine, management, law or business. It is vital to have lots of "salty" Christians who are bringing up families, serving customers in stores and restaurants, policing the streets or building our homes. Every member of every church must fulfill his or her mission responsibilities in the area where God has placed him or her. The call to Sears is just as significant as the call to Africa! The crucial thing is to be a partner in mission wherever we are.

But in addition to this call on every Christian, some are called to exercise their gifts in specifically "Christian" activity—either in one's own country or abroad—through a church or mission agency. The need is great for dedicated missionaries of this kind, and particularly for those who will go to another culture, country or language group. Of all "full-time Christian workers," about 90 percent work in the privileged Western world, and only 10 percent work with the 90 percent of the global population in the rest of the world!

What causes reluctance to serve in full-time mission? There seem to be a number of factors—for example:

☐ Materialism has gripped the church as well as the world. There is a reluctance to accept a lower standard of living, which is often the consequence of working abroad.

☐ Mission abroad has a slightly dated, old-fashioned image. Long-term service with an established missionary agency can seem far less glamorous than many other ministry options.

☐ We live in an instant-results society. There is often great resistance to the years of language training and cultural orientation required for crosscultural service. We want to serve God *now!*

☐ The world we live in values tolerance above truth. There is an undercurrent of feeling in some churches that we have no right to interfere in the affairs of other countries. This is, to some extent, a reaction to our Western colonial past. It leaves even the most fervent believers wondering whether local Christians should be left to get on with the job of mission in their own countries.

No wonder mobilizing the church to release this kind of missionary is extremely difficult. Yet the need is so great. Over three thousand languages are without a Scripture translation, and almost two hundred major languages have not yet received the Christian message on the radio. About 40 percent of the world's population have never heard the gospel in a way they can understand, though many of us hear it several times a week. Can it be right that some have heard the message hundreds of times when there are millions who have never heard it once?

More than ever we need women and men to respond to the great challenge of world mission. That response will be costly in terms of family, health and comfort. It will demand dying to self and living for God—not in theory but in cold, hard practice.

When James Calvert sailed as a missionary to the cannibals of the Fiji Islands, the captain of the ship urged him not to go ashore: "You will lose your life and the lives of those with you if you go among such savages." Calvert replied, "We died before we came here."

In 1839 John Williams, with his wife, went to the cannibals of New Hebrides in the South Pacific. After a short period of service there they were both clubbed to death. Eighteen years later, in 1857, G. N. Gordon and his wife went to the islands, only to be murdered in 1861. John Paton followed a few years later, and the first Communion service, with twelve converts, was held in 1869.

Such courage and commitment are needed among us today. Cannibals may be rarer now, but the cost of missionary service can still be very high.

It is very important not to minimize the personal cost of missionary obedience. In human terms it can be a risky decision with the potential to adversely affect family, career, comfort and health. An ad that appeared some years ago in Great Britain sums it up:

Ability to mix with people, mix concrete, wade rivers,

write articles, love one's neighbor, deliver babies, sit cross-legged, drain swamps, digest questionable food, patch human weakness, suffer fools gladly and burn the midnight oil—these are required for service!

Persons allergic to ants, babies, beggars, chop suey, cockroaches, curried crabs, duplicators, guitars, humidity, indifference, itches, jungles, mildew, minority groups, mud, poverty, sweat and unmarried mothers had better think twice before applying! Who will take up this challenge? Will you go as God calls? You may not think you are holy enough, old enough, young enough, clever enough, healthy enough, wise enough or even bothered enough—but are you willing enough?

And don't be fooled into believing some of the common myths about missionaries.

Most of the basic qualifications for missionary service abroad or far afield are related to character. (In the next chapter we will look at some of the practical steps and training required.) Humility, patience and the ability to control your temper may be as valuable to you in God's service as a knowledge of New Testament Greek or a thorough grasp of missiology.

On one occasion a mission agency decided to test an applicant's character in an unusual way. At 3:00 on a cold morning the candidate walked into the agency's office for a scheduled interview with the personnel director. He waited until 8:00 a.m., when the director finally arrived.

The personnel director sat down with him and said, "First, spell *Baker*."

"B-A-K-E-R," the young man said.

Common myths about missionaries

Myth 1: Missionaries always have a dramatic "call."

They don't! Moses did, and so did the apostle Paul (Exodus 3; Acts 9), but lots of missionaries simply had a gradual and growing conviction that God wanted them to serve in this way.

Myth 2: Missionaries never yell at their kids.

Of course this is true . . . and so are the facts that the Republicans advocate tax increases, the pope is a Jehovah's Witness and the Chicago Bulls have never won an NBA championship! Actually, missionaries have all the struggles associated with being a human and a Christian. Perfection is not a requirement.

Myth 3: Missionaries are naturally adventurous.

Usually rugged types, they enjoy poor sanitation, consider large spiders their friends and would give anything to experience malaria! In reality, the opposite is often the case. God gives courage as the need arises, not normally in advance. Throughout church history God has used weak and frail people in some of the toughest situations. (Note: there may be a biblical principle here: see 2 Corinthians 12:9-10!)

Myth 4: Missionaries are good at public speaking.

Many agricultural, medical and administrative missionaries don't have this gift. (Nor do some of the preachers!) Most people improve in this area with practice, but for many mission workers it is not a major component of what they do.

"Very good. Now let's see what you know about figures. How much is two times two?"

"Four," replied the applicant.

"Very good," the personnel director said. "I'll recommend that you be appointed. You have passed the test."

At the next meeting of the candidacy committee, the

personnel director spoke highly of the applicant: "He has all the qualifications of a missionary. Let me explain. First, I tested him on self-denial. I told him to be at my office at three in the morning. He left a warm bed and came out in the cold without a word of complaint. Second, I tried him out on punctuality. He appeared on time. Third, I examined him on patience. I made him wait five hours to see me. Fourth, I tested him on temper. He failed to show any sign of it; he didn't even question my delay. Fifth, I tried his humility. I asked him questions that a small child could answer, and he showed no offense. He meets the requirements and will make the missionary we need."

Hudson Taylor's qualifications for a missionary

☐ A life yielded to God and controlled by his Spirit
☐ A restful trust in God for the supply of all needs
☐ A sympathetic spirit and a willingness to take a lowly place
☐ Tact in dealing with people and adaptability in various circumstances
☐ Zeal in service and steadfastness in discouragement
☐ Love for communion with God and for the study of his Word
☐ Some experience and blessing in the Lord's work at home
☐ A healthy body and a vigorous mind

So will you go? Go next door or to the office of a colleague down the hall? Go across town or across the world? Go to a relative, a friend or a total stranger?

"How long will you waver between two opinions? If the LORD is God, follow him" (1 Kings 18:21).

Lifeguards on a beach in Jacksonville, Florida, must always be alert because of a strong but unseen undertow. Many times a week they dive into the water to rescue someone who appears to be struggling. Sometimes the swimmer would have managed without help; sometimes a life is saved or serious injury prevented. A huge sign in red letters hangs on the wall of the lifeguard station: "IF IN DOUBT, GO!" Perhaps this should be on the wall of every church building—and etched onto the heart of every church member.

John Mott, a missionary statesman, gave his whole life to building up the church's commitment to mission. His first official international involvement came when he was twenty-three years old, and this continued in various ways until he was well into his eighties. At the close of an address urging people to put world evangelism high on their personal agenda, he called out, "In view of the constraining memories of the cross of Christ and the love with which he has loved us, let us rise and resolve, at whatever cost of self denial, that live or die, we shall live or die for the evangelization of the world in our day."

Will we go in our day, as John Mott did in his?

Study Guide

Read Isaiah 6:1-8; Jeremiah 1:4-10.

1. Both Isaiah and Jeremiah felt inadequate in the face of God's call. What enabled them to fulfill their call? In what ways do you identify with them?

2. As a group, list as many things as you can that all

Christians are "called" to. Which of these relate to taking the good news about Jesus to others?

3. "Who will take up this challenge . . . are you willing enough?" (p. 55). Is being willing to go enough? Why or why not?

4. Hudson Taylor's list (p. 57) and 2 Corinthians 12:9-10 might suggest that most, if not all, Christians could be missionaries. Do you agree with this? Why or why not?

Chapter Five

Ready to Go?

In encouraging young people to come out as mission-aries, do use the greatest caution. One wrong-minded, obstinate person would ruin us. Humble, quiet, persevering folk of sound, sterling character, with good accomplishment and some natural aptitude to acquire a language; people with an amiable, yielding temper, willing to take the lowest place; who live close to God and who are willing to suffer all things for Christ's sake without being proud of it—these are the kind of people we need.
ANN JUDSON, pioneer missionary to Burma

*I*f you have been convinced that you should go, what is the next step? Quite a few people are challenged by a missionary speaker, at a conference or even by a book like this—but that's as far as it goes. Emotions of the heart must result in inquiry of the mind and activity of the body!

And even if your mission is not to be employed full time by a local church or Christian organization, this chapter is still for you. Remember, every Christian is called.

Growing

As you go, grow. Work hard to ensure that you have the essentials of Christian discipleship in place. Good foundations are essential in our lives as we think about building something of God into other people's.

It's good to have a basic understanding of the structure and general content of the books of the Bible. A simple grasp of what the Bible teaches about prayer, salvation, assurance, guidance, the church and evangelism is a good foundation for whatever God may guide you to in the future.

Consider going through a discipleship study guide with a friend. You could ask one of your church leaders for help or visit a Christian bookstore where the manager will be able to advise you. (You might want to ask about the Christian Basics Bible Study series or the Teamwork Discipleship Guides from InterVarsity Press.) Even if you have been a Christian for years, a refresher course in these areas would be a good idea.

Thinking

What is God calling you to do? If you feel you may be experiencing a specific call to missionary employment, some of these next suggestions will be particularly appropriate. Others who are concerned about missions will find them helpful to consider as well.

My first suggestion is to think and pray about what God may be calling you to. Certain attitudes toward Christian service are unhelpful. "Full-time" Christian work is not somehow superior to secular work. Missionaries and pastors are not God's special favorites. IBM is as much a mission field as Asia! But the opposite attitude is also wrong. "Full-time" service need not be an escape into a religious ghetto or a retreat for weak people from the pressures of the world. The fact that it is an escape for some does not mean it is so for everybody.

World mission is the responsibility of every believer, but we will not all fulfill our responsibility in the same way. Careful thought must be given to how and where we are to be God's mission agents—our obedience is the important thing. We are in the right place, doing the right thing, when we are doing God's thing in God's place!

One day Wilfred Grenfell, medical missionary to Labrador, was a guest at a dinner in London along with a number of socially prominent British men and women. During the course of the dinner, the lady seated next to him turned and said, "Is it true, Dr. Grenfell, that you are a missionary?" Grenfell looked at her for a moment before replying, "Is it true, madam, that you are not?"

Exploring
There are quite a few things you can do to begin to explore what God may be calling you to. You could start by sitting down to discuss the matter with your minister or other church leaders. Listen carefully to what they say. They may have a more objective view of your character and gifts, which it will be helpful to hear (though perhaps not always enjoyable!). Don't be discouraged if they appear slightly negative about your desire to serve God. Remember that they may have been drawn into many similar conversations that did not result in any action. Any less-than-enthusiastic

response may simply reflect a concern to see how serious you really are about all this.

It is vital to check out any sense of call with a responsible church leader. Some people can be extremely certain about their call—but wrong! Some are very uncertain and need help in clarifying things. We need the wisdom and insight of others.

It can also be valuable to talk to a missionary who is home on leave, or fax or phone a mission worker abroad

---

Application form for short-term mission work

Name

Address

Date of birth

Marital status

Describe your educational background and academic qualifications.

List your previous employers and work experience.

How did you become a Christian?

What church do you attend?

What Christian work have you been involved in?

How would you describe your state of health?

Provide two references (one from the minister of your church) in support of your application.

This is a summary of half a dozen application forms from various Christian organizations. If you are applying for long-term service, the questions will be more extensive and more detailed. If you hope to work with children, you will also be asked questions about any criminal convictions you have had and whether or not you are willing to submit to a background check. You will probably be asked to supply a couple of passport-size photographs of yourself.

---

to find out how they became convinced about their call to this sort of Christian service. Or you could try interviewing a pastor in your area who is from a different denomination. Different traditions see the call to service in different ways, and it can be useful to be exposed to other approaches.

Begin to subscribe to a couple of missionary magazines—one dealing with work at home and one with work abroad. (See the resource section at the end of the book.) Do they describe anything that you could contribute to or would enjoy? As you pray about what you read, God may show you possible future roles.

Working

Going abroad is unlikely to turn you into a Christian worker! "Work where you are, so you can work where you're sent" is a good motto. Another is "If you won't be missed, don't go!" Being a loyal church member and a faithful participant in local church life is vitally important.

"Lone rangers" rarely last long overseas. Committed participation in the local body of Christ *now* will enable spiritual development and may help ensure that you don't make big mistakes in your exploration of God's will. And your minister will be able to write you a good reference for a missionary agency if he has already seen you at work in the church!

There are other areas of Christian work you can explore as you test the waters of God's call. Some missionary agencies offer opportunities to do short-term work (anything from two weeks to two years) in countries where they operate. To do this you may be able to take time off work, use part of your vacation or

Short-term mission: pros and cons

Pros

1. Gives vision of the need in other countries.
2. Requires no expensive language study.
3. No need to bring much luggage, no [moving] expenses.
4. Can witness to those who speak English, or through an interpreter.
5. No family who has to travel with you.
6. No long-term investment—if you fall ill, you can be sent home.
7. Opportunity to test call.
8. Effective in restricted countries, *e.g.*, Turkey or Iran.
9. Generates interest in home churches.
10. Many short-termers come back as long-termers.
11. Many become lifelong supporters of missions.

Cons

1. Inexperience. No gradual introduction possible.
2. No language (cannot answer telephone or read time-table).
3. Clueless about culture even when interpreted.
4. No time to build long-term relationships for evangelism.
5. No time to plant churches.
6. Short-term projects may siphon off funds from long-term ones.
7. Distraction for long-termers asked for assistance.

Short-term work is very useful for the participants in gaining a vision of the great need of the world for the gospel.

Michael Griffiths, Tinker, Tailor, Missionary? *(Leicester, U.K.: Inter-Varsity Press, 1992), p. 127*

put to use a period between jobs. People taking early retirement may have a huge amount to contribute. You might participate in a spring-break beach mission, a building crew or an evangelism team. Quite a few organizations set up these activities and will send you their literature (see the list at the back of the book).

"Tentmaker" versus traditional missionary

Countries with no restrictions on entry allow two options: full-time missionary or professional overseas "tentmaker."

Full-time missionary

Pros

1. Allows full-time activity as evangelist and church-planter.
2. Allows setting aside adequate time for language learning.
3. Allows close integration with national church.
4. Suited to those who can do one thing well at a time.

Cons

1. May be despised as a religious professional.
2. Is barred from entering some countries.
3. Cannot witness through daily work.

Professional overseas "tentmaker"

Pros

1. Attracts respect as making a secular contribution.
2. May reach "high level" people socially.
3. Can witness through daily work.
4. Costs nothing to the sending church.
5. May be generously salaried and therefore able to support Christian work on the spot from personal income.

Cons

1. May never achieve skills in foreign language.

2. May be isolated in expatriate ghetto.
3. May have to join segregated expatriate church.
4. Has only limited time for church work.
5. Requires higher spiritual gifts than a full-timer.
Countries with no entry or visas for missionaries allow one option: part-time "tentmaker."

Part-time "tentmaker"
This Christian is admitted because of professional skills in medicine, teaching, business or diplomacy. He or she witnesses by the quality of his or her daily work, by taking opportunities in the course of it, and in free time, sometimes under restrictions not to "proselytize." It demands probably a higher measure of spiritual gift than a professional missionary, because of the limited time available. And at the home end, it requires at least as much moral and prayer support.
Michael Griffiths, Tinker, Tailor, Missionary? (Leicester, U.K.: Inter-Varsity Press, 1992), pp. 69-70

Maturing

Being part of a Christian organization or church staff is not always as easy at it might appear. Any image you have of sitting around all day singing choruses, studying Bible passages and having lots of fellowship time should be erased from your mind! Just as in any other workplace, you could encounter bad tempers, gossip and fragile egos. It takes real maturity not to become cynical when you work with God's people!

Good relationship skills are very important in the task of mission. You may be called on to relate to mission workers from other countries, national Christians and church leaders, and the non-Christian residents of the area you are working in—all in the "pressure cooker" atmosphere of unfamiliar cuisine, culture, customs and climate. Add to this the fact that you are not feeling too well, that you are tired and homesick. Will you have the maturity to be a calm, positive influence in such an environment? I accept that even the archangel Gabriel might fail this particular test, but the principle is important. Emotional maturity is an important feature of successful, long-lasting survival in the task of mission.

Another important aspect of maturity is discipline—discipline in the use of time and money in particular. Christian workers often have to take a great deal of responsibility for setting their own work schedule. Either of the opposite evils of laziness and workaholism will not serve you well in Christian service. At one end of the spectrum you will kill God's work, and at the other end it will kill you! One's use of money can reveal your character. Embrace generosity but avoid waste; and of course, scrupulous honesty in financial matters is essential.

Maturity in sexual relationships is another crucial area. Sexual indiscretion is, sadly, too common among Christian workers. This of course discredits the gospel and damages both the people and the agency for which they work. Coming to terms with your own sexuality is a necessary facet of preparation for mission work.

All this talk about maturity could drive you to despair. Maturity, after all, can't be studied for or discovered at a conference. The important thing is *movement* toward maturity. We can reflect prayerfully on our life's experiences and make progress in maturity: *becoming* more self-aware, *becoming* more aware of how we affect others, *becoming* more disciplined, and so on. This process can be strengthened when we have an honest friend who will tell us the truth in love. A prayer partner, a spiritual director or a discipler could fulfill this role.

> So far in the history of the world there have never been enough mature people in the right places.
> *George B. Chisholm*
>
> Mature people are made not out of good times but out of bad times.
> *Hyman Judah Schachtel*
>
> The discipline of desire is the background of character.
> *John Locke*
>
> One of the marks of a mature person is the ability to dissent without creating dissension.
> *Don Robinson*
>
> Maturity begins to grow when you can sense your concern for others outweighing your concern for yourself.
> *John MacNaughton*

Learning

You can't become a brain surgeon overnight! Training and experience are essential. Similarly, whatever skills you bring to Christian work, additional training is almost always appropriate.

It can be useful to read some Christian biographies, but do make sure you read accounts of missionaries from the last few decades, such as Jackie Pullinger, Chet Bitterman or Thomas Hale, as well as from the last two centuries. If a book paints a picture of a Christian hero with no flaws and tells a story of uninterrupted success—get another book!

It is important to learn more about the area you feel God may be calling you to. We are all called to the world, so we ought to take steps to learn more about the way it works. Read a newspaper and perhaps a newsmagazine; keep abreast of world news as well as national-interest stories. If you feel called to work among young people, for example, begin to ask questions about what influences and motivates them. Look at the magazines they read, listen to their music, interview a teacher, even talk to a teenager! If you feel called to a specific country or continent, find out about its population mix, politics, geography, church life and culture. Most good libraries will provide material on this, and some excellent material is available in Patrick Johnstone's *Operation World* (Grand Rapids, Mich.: Zondervan, 1993).

Features of the Western world

☐ Objective truth is replaced by the view that we have to construct our own truths (relativism).

☐ Blurring of distinctions such as right and wrong, people and machines, people and animals, male and female, the real world and virtual reality, fantasy and reality, God and nature.

☐ Search for the transcendent. The magical, mysterious and mystical offer a powerful attraction.

☐ Nature becomes sacred Mother Nature. A new paganism is establishing itself.

☐ Loss of hope and idealism. People no longer look optimistically to the future. Nostalgia is evident (in popular music and fashion, for example).

If you get involved in a short-term project (say, for a few weeks), the agency you have applied to will provide some kind of orientation or training. Once you get involved in a commitment to a longer-term period of service, the training requirement will be more extensive. You may be asked to undergo a

Some worldwide trends

☐ *Economic.* Increase in economic disparity and other injustices between rich and poor—within nations and between nations.

☐ *Social and political.* Two major forces are more and more in conflict: unification and fragmentation. Technology and the media contribute to an increasing standardization of lifestyle throughout the world. At the same time, there is an increase in nationalism, ethnic awareness, minority group solidarity and individualism.

☐ *Population.* There is a dramatic shift to urban dwelling throughout the world, with a subsequent rise in megacities. In many part of the world the majority of the population are children or young people. The family is disintegrating under pressures of modern change as well as moral decline.

☐ *Environmental.* Modern social change in lifestyle is resulting in an environmental crisis unprecedented in history. Our grandchildren and great-grandchildren may accuse twentieth-century people of being "ecological criminals."

☐ *Religions.* World religions are in revival and cults are on the increase at the beginning of a new millennium. Within the Christian church there has been a shift in the center of gravity from the West to the Two-Thirds World in church growth.

period of theological education as well as language and "culture-shock" preparation. Be prepared to spend years, rather than months, getting ready for some types of missionary work.

And of course it is best to plan on a lifetime of learning and training. The best Christian workers are always trying to enhance their skills and develop their understanding. Sabbaticals, study leave, conferences and keeping up to date with reading are all features of a mission worker who wants to make a significant long-term contribution to his or her area of work.

Praying

> God's acquaintance is not made hurriedly. He does not bestow His gifts on the casual, or hasty comer or goer. To be much alone with God is the secret of knowing Him and of influence with Him.
> *E. M. Bounds*

Prayer is an indispensable part of your preparation for a life of service. Through prayer God can confirm, for example, what part of the world you should serve him in and what you should be doing when you get there.

Regular conversations with God make us familiar with his voice and therefore more sensitive to his direction.

Without listening to God, many of us are prone to rush headlong into the wrong thing. Or the inadequacy of our prayer is revealed in an almost permanent indecision. China? Africa? New York City? The destina-

tion changes weekly, on the basis of the last missionary speaker we heard or the last missionary biography we read. A sermon on being salt and light at
work convinces us to get a "normal" job at the
bank; a TV documentary on African hunger sends
us scurrying to get an application form from Food
for the Hungry.

Faithful prayer, patient waiting on God, can give us
a quiet, growing certainty about the call of God on our
lives. Good decisions flow more readily when God has

The Top Ten

The top ten missionary-sending countries of the non-
Western world in 1988 were as follows (the numbers
indicate active missionaries):
India: 8,905
Nigeria: 2,595
Zaire: 2,731
Burma: 2,560
Kenya: 2,242
Brazil: 2,040
Philippines: 1,814
Ghana: 1,545
Zimbabwe: 1,540
Korea: 1,184
Source: Robin Thomson, World Christian *(Oxford: Lynx/St John's
Extension Studies, 1992)*

been allowed, in a paraphrase of a well-known hymn,
to "drop his still dews of quietness, till all our strivings
cease, taking from our souls the strain and stress, until
our ordered lives confess the beauty of his peace."

But prayer is vital for another important reason as

The modern story of world mission

The modern story began in the nineteenth century. Here are just a few examples.

☐ *Burma and Thailand.* Back in 1833, the Karens of Burma, who had only recently been evangelized, began outreach to the Kachin, a very different people, as well as to other Karens in Thailand. The Burma Baptist Convention is still the largest single missionary agency in Asia.

☐ *Tongans* planted the church in Fiji in 1835. Their king sent a message to the paramount chief of Fiji, preparing the way for a group of Tongan missionaries! British missionaries joined the partnership later in the same year. Well over 1,000 missionaries have been sent between the many islands of the Pacific since then, many traveling from island to island in their deep-sea canoes.

☐ *Jamaicans* began missionary work in Cameroon in 1893. They started Bible translation, printing and education. Today Caribbean Christians from Britain continue to work in Ghana, Nigeria, Liberia and other West African countries.

☐ *Latin American* countries have been sending missionaries within their continent, as well as to Spain, Portugal and the USA. COMIBAM, a congress on mission in São Paulo in 1987, gave a new push to send missionaries outside the continent. There is a special interest in working in the Muslim countries of North Africa and the Middle East.

A Brazilian girl heard about Asians from Hindu and Muslim backgrounds. She came to London to learn English and is now working with Asians in Manchester [England].

☐ *India.* India's missionary movement goes back to 1884, when the Methodist Church sent a missionary to Singapore. The Indian Missionary Society was founded in 1903, followed soon after by the National Missionary

Society. Both are still active. But the explosion of missionary growth began in the fifties and sixties. Individuals, churches and small groups began to go, or dream about going, to unreached areas of north India. "Go or Send" was the motto of one of the groups. Today their efforts have grown into thousands of cross-cultural workers all over India, and abroad as well. A marine biologist from Madras left his research to work with students in Thailand. Teachers have gone to Fiji and other Pacific Islands, medical workers to Afghanistan, evangelists and pastors to Britain.

□ *Japan.* In the 1960s three young Japanese went to India for theological study. Their purpose: to learn another language and culture and prepare for overseas missionary work. They went back to Japan, married three sisters and scattered again to work in India and the Caribbean. Other Japanese work today in Kenya, Indonesia, Nepal, Thailand, Britain, and at least 20 other countries.

□ *Korea.* A Korean girl works in London with Bengali Muslims and Burmese Buddhists. A theological student is now pastor to Korean businessmen in Bombay. A dentist has a clinic and plans for a dental college in Northern China. Koreans in the Middle East make an impression with their early morning prayer meetings.

□ *Africans* cross national and cultural boundaries within their continent. Kenyan students in India have a powerful witness. Nigerians and Ghanaians in Britain evangelize the local people. The East African Revival has ministered to people all around the world.

Robin Thomson, World Christian (Oxford: Lynx/St John's Extension Studies, 1992)

well. God wants to tell us not only where to go and what to do, but how to *be.* That is, God is more concerned about our character than about our career. From his point of view, our geographical location and specific job description are less important than the Christlikeness of our lives. Prayerful, Jesus-centered people can make an impact for God almost anywhere; prayerless people do mess things up for God almost everywhere!

When we put prayer first, we join with thousands of Christian men and women throughout history who have been used by God to accomplish great things in his name. There is no more important preparation for Christian service than having our character progressively made like that of Jesus through the ministry of prayer.

J. C. Ryle, a bishop of Liverpool in the nineteenth century, summed it up like this: "I have read the leaves of many eminent Christians who have been on earth since the Bible days. Some of them, I see, were rich, and some were poor. Some were learned, some unlearned. Some have loved to use a liturgy, and some choose to use none. But one thing, I see, they all had in common. They all have been people of prayer."

Study Guide
Read Colossians 1:9-12, 28-29; 2:6-8. Then reread the section "Maturing" (pp. 68-70).

1. Identify marks of maturity from the Colossians passages. How can you, as a group, specifically promote each other's growth in these areas?

2. Are there any areas in which you would particularly like to develop? (See leader's note 1, p. 114, at the back of this book.)

3. What is the difference between being an "older" Christian and being a "more mature" Christian?

4. On page 68 we read, "Good relationship skills are very important in the task of mission." Identify at least six such skills. In what ways can you develop these skills?

5. Is your group particularly strong or weak in any of these skills? Discuss your views about this together.

Chapter Six

A Mission-Minded Church

*Foreign missions are not an extra; they are the acid
test of whether or not the church believes the gospel.*
LESSLIE NEWBIGIN

*H*ow can we get mission onto the agenda of the
local church? What should we do to give a higher priority to the task of supporting mission
workers, being a mission-centered church and produc-
ing interest in mission in our children and young
people?

Budget

Putting our money where our mouth is—that's a good
place to start. Many churches have taken huge strides
forward by making a significant faith-decision about
missionary giving. Some set a "goal per member": that
is, they pledge to give, say, seventy-five dollars per
member per year to mission from the general fund (in

other words, one hundred members would generate seventy-five hundred dollars each year). Other churches decide to give away a percentage of their annual income. They may start by giving 10 percent and plan to increase this by a further 10 percent each year until, after five years, they are giving half their income to "outside causes." Others go for more modest increases.

However it is done, it should be done! Only by giving decisively and generously can we avoid failing in our financial responsibilities in this area. "In-house" needs will always be present, but we must resist using the mission budget to help balance the books. For many churches, announcing a minimum figure that will be given away is the only way to ensure that other claims don't eat into the mission budget each year.

It's not unknown for a church treasurer to delay payment to a missionary agency until the next financial year, or not to send it at all, when he or she is having trouble balancing the books. So it is essential for local churches to move mission giving from the "might pay" to the "must pay" category.

Systematic, planned mission budgeting also helps avoid "panic" or "emotional" giving when a crisis occurs. Special collections may have their place, but there are quickly diminishing returns if they are done too frequently. What's more, they tend to link mission support to a knee-jerk crisis mentality of giving. Mission should be supported because it is *right* to do all year round, not just because a big story hits our TV screens or a mission agency writes of a "cash flow" crisis or a once-in-a-lifetime opportunity.

Leadership in Mission

Churches tend to reflect the priorities of their leaders. Whenever the pastor is enthusiastic about mission, there is a good chance that the church will catch the vision.

In an ideal situation, the leaders will be committed to seeing all of church life exposed to mission. This rescues mission from being simply the responsibility of yet another committee or pressure group in the church. It is, rather, the "salt" of church life, flavoring everything—or as a great Swiss theologian, Emil Brunner, put it, "The church exists by mission, as fire exists by burning."

Whether or not the pastor of a church is positive about mission, the appointment of a missions coordinator or missions pastor can be very helpful. This individual should use every opportunity to stimulate interest in mission.

Supporting Missionaries

If someone has gone from your church family to do Christian service—whether at home or abroad—you will want to support them as well as possible. If no one has gone from your church you can adopt a mission worker serving in a part of the world you want to pray for. A mission agency can help provide you with a missionary to sponsor.

Either way, the mission worker you are linked with will want to know that he or she is supported in *prayer*—not just promises of prayer, but the real thing! One of the saddest stories I have heard was about a missionary couple and their young child who felt called

A mission coordinator in the church could draw people into missions awareness and commitment in many ways.

☐ Lead a monthly prayer meeting to pray for specific projects, organizations or countries. This prayer group could also be an action group, helping with mission events.

☐ Write articles on mission for the church magazine. Review books about mission; if the church has a bookstore, ask that these books be stocked.

☐ Arrange an evening meal based on food from different countries. Pray for the countries. Have information sheets available on the tables. Play music from another culture. Have the waiters in national costumes. Write the menu in various languages. With some imagination, this can be a very enjoyable evening and can significantly affect prayer for and interest in missions.

☐ Put up a mission display board. Give information about a missionary or a country. List items for praise and needs for prayer. Lots of big pictures, a map, diagrams and bright colors are ideal. Keep it simple and uncluttered, with not too many words in small type. Change it every month if you can. Be as professional as possible.

☐ Keep the church's small groups informed. Send missions material to small group leaders from time to time, offering information and requesting prayer. Then try to let them know how their prayers were answered!

☐ Ask the leaders for a prayer and information time during occasional Sunday services. Be brief, specific and interesting—especially if you want to be allowed to do it again! Use the overhead projector, show a piece of clothing from the country you are describing, or bring a national flag. Encourage your leaders to address some aspect of mission whenever God's people get together.

☐ See if you can arrange a missions weekend. This could involve Saturday workshops on mission-related topics. A guest speaker could be invited for the subsequent Sunday services. Decorate the church with a variety of national flags. Learn a song or hymn from another country. Have a number of displays featuring the work of various mission agencies.

□ Consider twinning your church with another fellowship in a completely different part of the world. You could exchange newsletters, prayer concerns and even pastors (temporarily!) to ensure greater understanding of the world church. You could send money or personnel to help support them in specific projects.

to a particularly difficult part of Africa. Their whole church covenanted to pray for them—especially regarding the threat to their lives from disease and marauding gangs. After less than two years the little boy and his mother died of a virulent local fever, and the husband too became infected. He was rushed back to his home country in a last-ditch attempt to save his life.

Discharged from the hospital—for there was little the doctors could do—he arrived late for the church's prayer meeting. Slipping in at the back, he sat unnoticed through the whole meeting. There were prayers for many aspects of church life, but not a mention was made of him or his situation, despite the letters he had sent urging prayer for his family in crisis. He slipped out quietly into the night, forgotten by everyone but God. He died within days, a broken man, a brother betrayed by unkept promises. This is a stark reminder to say what we mean and mean what we say about praying for mission workers.

And, of course, mission workers need to be sup-

> Unprayed for I feel like a diver at the bottom of a river
> with no connecting airline to the surface, or like a
> fireman wielding an empty hose on a burning building.
> With prayer I feel like David facing Goliath.
> *James Gilmour, missionary to Mongolia*

ported *financially*. If there is a sending agency (such as
a missionary society or evangelistic organization),
some discussion will need to take place with them.
What level of support is needed? How long is the
appointment for? What happens if the money runs out?
Whatever the precise details of the arrangements, the
local church will want to be as generous as possible.

Missionaries also need *contact* support. They could
be sent tapes of recent sermons, the church newsletter and perhaps a monthly rundown of key developments in church life. Church members should be
encouraged to write, fax or phone, as appropriate.
From time to time a significant new Christian book
could be mailed to them, or the latest tape of worship
songs. Think of what you would miss if you lived for
a long period abroad. Would they appreciate a subscription to a sports or hobby magazine? a newspaper? a supply of M&Ms? Try especially to remember
birthdays and anniversaries. Be creative and energetic in discovering and meeting these personal
needs. An item taken for granted here in the West can
make a huge difference to someone thousands of miles
away from home.

The key to supporting workers in mission—in prayer,
finance and contact—is consistency. Mission support
is a marathon, not a sprint. "Little and often" is a much

better approach than overwhelming support for two months followed by two years of virtual silence.

When they come home

☐ Welcome returning missionaries with enthusiasm. Make them feel appreciated and loved. Perhaps you should send a welcoming committee to the airport. But give them space to get over jet lag and reacclimate to life back home.

☐ Give thought to questions related to where they might live while on home assignment and their need for a car—before they come home! Will they need extra money while they are home?

☐ Give them an early and significant opportunity to address the church with a word of greeting and news highlights. After a few weeks an opportunity can be arranged for a fuller report and time set aside to pray. Let them tell their story.

☐ Things have changed during their absence! The church might consider appointing a (discreet, gentle and thoughtful) "caregiver" to provide appropriate phone numbers, directions to new facilities, escorts for shopping outings and so on.

☐ Be sensitive! Coming home can be a huge emotional adjustment. Meeting up with family they may not have seen for a couple of years, the sadness of missing colleagues on the mission field, feeling overwhelmed by the affluence of the West compared with where they have been . . . these, and many other things, can be quite a shock to the system.

☐ What do they enjoy doing at home that it is hard to do abroad? Watching Big Eight football games? Seeing a play? Visiting an amusement park? Perhaps the church could find out and provide the money and contacts to make it happen.

☐ Why not suggest (and pay for!) a complete medical examination for the missionary family? a visit to the dentist? an optician's appointment? Health care overseas—especially in remote areas—is not always good, and you do want to send your Christian workers back in the best possible shape!

☐ Representatives of the leadership should meet with returning workers to discuss support and links with their sending agency and to give both sides time to reflect on how to strengthen missionary-church connections. There may be unrealized expectations and frustrations on either side. Honesty, love and sensitivity will be needed.

☐ Try to treat them "normally." Make sure they are included in routine church life—not as special guests, just as part of the family. Don't give them a special welcome at every meeting or fuss over them in an unnaturally gushing way. This can appear to be condescending or patronizing—"our sweet little missionary family!"

☐ Give them the opportunity to attend refresher courses and to engage in extra study to prepare for their next term of service.

☐ Send them back with prayer, perhaps in a special service of recommissioning. Give a small gift to each member of the family as a reminder of the love and prayers of the people back home. Arrange for them to be taken to the airport.

A Mission Church: Today and Tomorrow

It is vital to infect future generations with the mission-enthusiasm bug! Our children's program and activities should reflect a passion for world mission. Returning Christian workers should not be be viewed as the exclusive property of the "adult church." Simple concepts illustrated with striking visual aids can draw even very young children into the world of mission. Perhaps a serving missionary could write a "child-friendly" newsletter, or the grownups' version could be adapted by a children's worker. Curriculum materials should include illustrations from other cultures. Some mission agencies produce magazines for children, and these can be circulated and could form part of a lesson in children's church or Sunday school.

Many churches have the world on their own doorstep! What about a joint session with the children from the Hispanic church down the road? Or a visit from an Asian-American children's choir? Experiences like these broaden our children's understanding of culture and Christian faith.

There is an important challenge here for the children's workers and helpers in our churches. We must take great care not to pass on to our children our own prejudices or misconceptions about people of other races and nationalities. Views implying cultural superiority or subtle racism are not unknown in our churches!

Where we have Christian parents, this is obviously the best place to foster world-mission awareness—in the home. We can make a point of entertaining missionaries for Sunday lunch whenever the opportunity arises. We can actively support all the mission emphases to which the church is trying to expose our children. If you get hold of a copy of Jill Johnstone's *You Can Change the World* (Grand Rapids, Mich.: Zondervan, 1993), you will be able to talk and pray with your children about dozens of different nations of the world. Children tend to pick up our values and priorities through the atmosphere of daily life in the home. What we give time to, spend money on and talk about sends signals that shape young lives.

Once children get to the allowance stage, it can be useful to encourage them to give a proportion to the church and another sum specifically for world mission. A map of the world in the hallway or a globe on top of the piano can be a useful visual reminder of life beyond the home country. Write a family letter to a mission worker, with each family member contributing. The youngest child could draw a picture or at least make a mark on the paper—a missionary family would relate to this correspondence with enthusiasm!

The church's role is to encourage parents to take seriously their world-mission responsibilities to their children. We may even be able to arrange a "missionary experience" at the church (such as displays, mission literature, food tasting, a makeshift "slum," border checkpoints, games) that adults and children can tour together. In the long term, we pray that our children will grow up with a world-mission focus firmly established as part of their Christian experience—ready, in turn, to pass on this commitment to mission to their own children.

Churches that do the kinds of things this chapter has described can make a significant contribution to global mission. Such churches also tend to make a significant impact locally. My observation over the years has been that when local congregations are absorbed with "external" needs, "internal" issues (such as worship and unity) are not major sources of contention. When a church is internally focused, however, mission is neglected and internal tensions absorb ever-increasing amounts of time and energy. Let's get our churches focused upward to God and outward to the world.

Study Guide
Read Philippians 1:3-5; 4:14-19.

1. Which of the ideas presented in this chapter do you think would be good for you, your family or your church to adopt? How can you make progress in this?

2. Reread the section "Supporting Missionaries" (pp. 81-85). How could your group be directly involved in this?

3. Imagine that a missionary from your church has just returned from ten years in Nepal. What cultural changes will they encounter? How can you make their reentry go more smoothly (pp. 85-86)?

4. The Philippian church stood out to Paul as giving good support. How do you think their support affected Paul? What did they lose or gain by supporting him in the way they did?

5. To what extent is your church internally focused or externally focused (pp. 88-89)? What can you and your group do to become more externally focused?

Chapter Seven

Heroes for a World in Need

*T*his is a very needy world. We learn this every time we watch the television news or listen to reports on the radio as we drive to work. Our eyes and ears are exposed daily to news of death, disease, war and famine. Greed on a global scale, searing anger and hatred between individuals and nations—an almost constant shroud of sadness seems to cover our broken world.

Of course there is also evidence of hope in the most unlikely places. Costly acts of kindness, self-sacrificing compassion and deep expressions of love—all these things exist in far greater abundance than one would guess from the national news. Some hungry people are fed, some homeless people are housed, and some defenseless people are protected. Christians are actively involved, with others, in these vital activities.

And the gospel is making inroads into our world. Each year about forty million people become Christians and some fifty thousand churches are planted. In parts of Africa the church is growing faster than the population. South Korea is on course for half its population to be Christian. On every continent (with the exception of Europe!) the church of Jesus seems to be growing. This information should encourage us, but not cause us to be complacent. These signs of hope should not obscure the size of the task that remains to be done.

Where are the lost?

☐ Most of those who have not heard the gospel are in the 10/40 window. This is an area from 10 degrees north latitude to 40 degrees north latitude, and covers much of northern Africa, the Arab world, India, China and Indonesia.

☐ This area has over 4 billion people, which includes 1 billion Muslims, 1 billion Hindus and 237 million Buddhists.

☐ 8 out of 10 of the world's poor live here.

☐ 50 of the least evangelized cities (1 million people plus) are in the window.

☐ It attracts only 20% of missionary resources.

Dave Roberts, Mission Possible (London: Evangelical Missionary Alliance/Alpha Magazine, 1994)

Around 40 percent of the population of planet Earth (approximately two billion people) have yet to hear the gospel in a way they can understand. Islam may be spreading at an even more rapid rate than Christianity, and Hinduism at an equal rate with the Christian faith.

Secularization continues to engulf the affluent West, with a consequent abandonment of traditional forms of Christianity. New Age teaching abounds, and cults continue to flourish. Ninety percent of preachers are working with the 10 percent of the world's population who speak English. Only 0.5 percent of full-time missionaries are working among people groups where the good news is completely unknown. There are still over three thousand languages with no access to any part of the Bible, and a quarter of all people groups don't have a meaningful church to be part of. Giving to missionary agencies is rising more slowly than inflation.

There is still a great deal to be done. Population growth alone presents us with a huge task to take us well into the twenty-first century. Much of this growth will be in China and India, where the gospel has not made ready progress.

Perhaps the task we face is not greater than in the past, but mission workers today face different problems. Transportation and communication, two of the greatest practical problems facing past generations of missionaries, are much easier today; almost everywhere physical danger, health risks and poor living conditions were more of a problem in times past than they are today. Separation from family and friends was for longer periods, sometimes indefinitely. Amy Carmichael was in India for fifty-three years without a break; William Carey *never* came home on furlough. Missionary news could take six months or longer to get back to the sending church. And don't forget, the concept of short-term missionary service is a very recent one. It became possible only with the arrival of

Mission at the turn of the millennium

Mission today is a million miles removed from images of pith helmets and mission compounds. What has changed?

National leadership. Mission groups seek to work themselves out of a job by relinquishing power as soon as possible to local leadership. This creates faster church growth, causes fewer communication problems and negates the possibility of unhealthy cultural imperialism.

Targeting people groups. There may be 251 nations in the world, but there are at least twelve thousand people groups with their own distinctive culture, customs and language forms. Five thousand of the least reached groups are in the 10/40 window (see p. 92). Pioneer crosscultural missionaries are still needed to help these groups. These pioneers will be needed for several decades as they seek to support local leaders with Bible and mission training.

Wholistic mission. While some mission groups emphasize church planting, others also emphasize that the kingdom of God means justice for the oppressed and food for the hungry. Many believe that there is not an either-or tension between these issues and that we need to both plant churches and promote justice.

The multicultural church. The meteoric rise of vibrant Christianity in Latin America, Korea and various other communities worldwide means that Western Christians no longer dominate the worldwide Christian community. Nonwhite believers are now in the worldwide majority. It's estimated that the 35,000 non-Western missionaries of the late 1980s will have multiplied to a 160,000 majority group in world mission by the year 2000.

Church to church. To help Western Christians retain a passion for mission, creative strategies of involvement are being pursued. Church twinning is bringing together churches like the Christian Fellowship Church in Belfast, Ireland, and the Tabernacle Church in Madrid, Spain. Some churches, if they're ready for the long haul, are getting involved in pioneer people-group evangelism. Often they work closely with a mission agency to help research mission opportunities during holidays, student visits and business trips to the relevant area. When a church has been established, they "twin" with the church and help support them in practical and spiritual ways. With a broad cross-section of the congregation involved in what is essentially a long-distance church plant, the needs of mission, and its impact, become very tangible to the home church.

World mission is alive and well. There's a commitment to cultural sensitivity and a desire to stay only as long as a missionary is needed. There's a passion for the lost and a passion for justice. There are ample opportunities for local Christians to think globally.

Dave Roberts, Mission Possible *(London: Evangelical Missionary Alliance/Alpha Magazine, 1994)*

relatively cheap passenger air travel.

Despite all this, women and men—heroes of the faith—did risk everything in response to the call of God to share the good news. Their lives, imperfections and all, have a good deal to teach us today.

Heroes Who Never Gave Up

I know exactly what you are going through because I am going through the same thing. . . . It seems as though everything I do is wrong and only my faith in a living God keeps me going, because I get one bang after another. (Gladys Aylward, pioneer missionary to China)

To read some biographies of missionaries you would think they arrived on foreign soil, led thousands to Christ, planted dozens of churches and died famous and appreciated. In reality, most godly missionaries are characterized by faithfulness and dogged stick-to-itive-ness—people who would never give up until God called them elsewhere or until they died.

William Carey endured incredible hardship in India. Peter, his five-year-old son, died. Dorothy, his wife, went mad and died. He remarried and his second wife died. His books were destroyed in a fire, including a translation of the Bible which he had to begin again.

C. T. Studd went as a missionary to China in 1885. After nine years, ill health forced him to return home. In 1900 he went to India, until sickness again took him back in Britain. In 1910 (contrary to medical advice) he went to Africa, where he worked until he died in 1931.

Amy Carmichael suffered a dislocated ankle, broken leg and twisted spine. So bad were these injuries that between 1931 (when the accident occurred) and 1939 she had only eight nights of sleep without the help of medication for the pain. And all the while she was running her children's home in India, suffering inter-mittent bouts of fever and neuralgia.

John Ryle, in his later ministry a very influential bishop of Liverpool, had to persist through many early trials. He spent his first years of ministry burdened with a huge family debt. His ministry was overshad-owed by an aggressive wealthy layman who wished to run the church, causing Ryle much heartache. During this same ministry he buried his first wife in 1847 and his second wife in 1860. Personal bereavement and professional hardship ran side by side.

More recently, Jackie Pullinger persevered for many years working with the hungry and the drug addicts of Hong Kong. The need was desperate, and there was so little that she felt she could do. Now there are teams reaching where she could not go.

As I write, "jungle missionaries" work in the Peruvian Amazon, staying one step ahead of terrorists, drug traffickers and oil men who are devastating jungle society and threatening its survival. National missionaries like Roger and Rebecca Márquez motivate tribal village churches for outreach. Native evangelists have preached the gospel in every one of the villages of the Shipibo tribe. Both Roger and Rebecca received a missionary calling to the Peruvian Amazon. The difficulties are great and the costs high—one native evangelist died from a poisonous snake bite while going to preach at an unreached village.

For all these people, faith and Christian ministry did not come easily. They proved the adage that "successful people are unsuccessful people who didn't give up." The mission task still needs people who will not give up!

President Theodore Roosevelt said, "Since becoming President, I have come to know that the finest of Americans we have abroad today are the missionaries of the Cross. I am humiliated that I am not finding out until this late day the worth of foreign missions and the nobility of the missionaries. Their testimony in China, for instance, during the war there, is beyond praise. Their courage is thrilling and their fortitude heroic."

Heroes in the Right Place—Eventually

We often imagine that guidance comes easily to those in Christian ministry. Don't they all have a hotline to heaven telling them where to work, when and how to get there? Actually they are often as confused as we are! David Livingstone first thought God was calling him to China—and then he went to Africa. William Carey felt he should serve God in Tahiti—and he ended up in India.

As for Thomas Barnado, he felt sure that God wanted him in China. He had come from Dublin to London to train as a missionary doctor. While in preparation to go he started a meeting for street children in the East End of London. After one of these meetings one of the poorest boys simply would not go home. Jim Jarvis finally told Barnado that he had no home to go to! Barnado could hardly believe it.

Soon after this he met Lord Shaftesbury at a dinner party and told him about the homelessness and poverty in the East End. Anthony Shaftesbury did not believe him until Barnado took him to a warehouse in Whitechapel. Here he encountered seventy-three boys living on their own. "Are you sure that it is to China God is sending you?" he asked Barnado.

Something clicked inside Thomas Barnado, and thereafter he devoted his life to the needy in London instead of China. This happened in 1866. In the thirty-nine years to his death his organization admitted 59,834 children to caring homes and helped a quarter of a million others.

China's loss was London's gain. Thank God that mission work is not closed to those who struggle with guidance, perhaps even getting it wrong at first.

Unlikely Heroes

Another myth about missionary "greats" is that somehow they had special advantages we lack. Wasn't Barnado from a wealthy, well-connected family? Wasn't John Wesley a graduate of Oxford University? Didn't C. T. Studd have the privilege of attending Eton and then Cambridge University? Yes, all this is true, but these are not necessarily typical. William Carey was a shoemaker with almost no formal education—what he learned he taught himself. Robert Moffat was an apprentice gardener who struggled to get himself accepted by a missionary society. He went on to have a huge impact in Africa and was the inspiration that drew David Livingstone to that country. Mary Slessor had a very difficult home life; her family was extremely poor, and her father was an alcoholic. She had very little education, yet God used her to have a profound impact in Nigeria—far greater than anyone could have ever thought possible, given her background. Her influence continues there to this day.

And what about Gladys Aylward? She had a significant impact in China, sharing the gospel, caring for the needy and looking after refugees. On one occasion she took over one hundred children on a two-hundred-mile journey over mountainous terrain to avoid capture by an invading army. And all this from a woman who had been consistently at the bottom of her class at school, had found employment only as a maid in a wealthy household and had been turned down by the missionary society she applied to, because they did not believe she would ever be able to learn Chinese.

The history of mission is a colorful history of "unlikely heroes," characterized by obedience rather than ability. Time after time God confirms his Word; "Think of what you were when you were called. Not many of you were wise by human standards; not many were influential; not many were of noble birth. But God chose the foolish things of the world to shame the wise; God chose the weak things of the world to shame the strong" (1 Corinthians 1:26-27).

What makes a hero?

The model of a hero for a Christian is the hero of heroes, Jesus, who, though he was God, voluntarily stripped himself of power, success and influence, steadfastly setting his face toward his sacrificial death in Jerusalem. He became a humble carpenter-builder, whose disciples were made up of fishermen and social outcasts.

The Bible is a gallery of unlikely heroes—men and women with obvious faults and feet of clay, who nevertheless had the courage to endure in faith. They had the character to overcome, sometimes intermittently, the limitations of their backgrounds, to renounce the ways of the powerful in favor of faith in God's plans, however foolish these plans seemed to the powerful (see Hebrews 11).

A contemporary writer who has effectively portrayed heroes with biblical qualities of humility, perseverance and character is J. R. R. Tolkien, best known for his Lord of the Rings series. His heroes include humble hobbits, half the height of humans, and a king with healing hands who disguises himself for many years as a wandering ranger. These heroes are guided by an unseen providence, and their self-sacrifice and renunciation of power outwits the dark power who holds the world in his sway.

Unsung Heroes

The history of mission is not primarily a story of "famous" people. Thousands of unknown women and men have laid down their lives in God's service. In fact, when God records the story of the world church, names you have never heard of will be given high profile and some "famous" Christians may hardly get a mention. For example, you have probably never heard of Edward Kimball, yet he set in process a remarkable chain of events because of his faithful "missionary" service.

Edward Kimball sold shoes for a living. He also happened to be Dwight Moody's Sunday-school teacher. One day in April 1858 he challenged Moody to give his life to Christ. Moody, who was working in his uncle's shop, gave his life to God in the basement storeroom. He grew up to give the same challenge to hundreds of thousands of others—on both sides of the Atlantic.

While preaching in England in 1879, Moody awakened the evangelistic passion of a pastor of a small church—his name was F. B. Meyer. Meyer came to America and saw a young student, Wilbur Chapman, won to the Lord. Chapman went to work for the Y.M.C.A. and asked Billy Sunday to help with evangelism. Having cut his teeth evangelistically at the Y.M.C.A., Sunday went on to hold an evangelistic campaign in Charlotte, North Carolina. It went so well that a follow-up mission was arranged, with Mordecai Hamm as the evangelist. It was during this mission that a sixteen-year-old boy made a public decision to follow Jesus. His name? Billy Graham. And Billy Graham has preached the good news to more people than anyone else in all of history.

Edward Kimball could not have known how incredibly strategic his conversation with Moody would turn out to be. It could be argued that all those converted under Billy Graham's ministry owe a debt to Edward Kimball. *Any one of us could be used to start a chain of events similar to this.*

> The evangelistic harvest is always urgent. The destiny of men and of nations is always being decided. Every generation is strategic. We are not responsible for the past generation, and we cannot bear the full responsibility for the next one; but we do have our generation. God will hold us responsible as to how well we fulfill our responsibilities to this age and take advantage of our opportunities.
> *Billy Graham*

John Staupitz and John Egglen are completely unknown to the vast majority of Christians—yet they were the ones who were instrumental in leading Martin Luther and Charles Spurgeon, respectively, to Christian faith. Unknown? Yes, but absolutely vital in the unfolding purposes of God. Unsung heroes? Yes, unsung by everyone except God!

George Verwer traces his conversion to an elderly woman's persistent prayers for his high school. He went on to inspire tens of thousands of young people of all abilities to short-term and long-term mission through Operation Mobilization.

There are thousands of others who have responded to God's call. These missionaries will never make it into the history books. You would be thrilled to know about Edwin, who at thirty-nine years of age was called by God to Colombia. A farmer who knew only two words of Spanish, he sold his farm and went to Colombia, staying for twenty years before he made a brief visit home. He has made a tremendous contribution for God. Then there is Dave, a social worker in England, and Valerie, a doctor, and Roger, an assembly-line worker, and Jane, a homemaker—the list goes on and on. These people all have a passion for mission, and I'm sure they have a place in God's book of "missionary greats."

Why not join them and become one of God's twenty-first-century heroes, allowing your life to be marked, like theirs, with the struggles and joys of being a servant and mission agent for God?

Study Guide
Read 1 Corinthians 1:26-27; Hebrews 12:1-4.

1. What impressed you as you read of the "heroes" mentioned in this chapter?

2. To what extent are these heroes ordinary, to what extent extraordinary?

3. What things do they have in common?

4. How can you develop individually and as a group in these areas?

5. Reread the story of Edward Kimball (p. 101-2). Do you think you could be an Edward Kimball? What can you do or pray, or ask others to do or pray, to help you be used by God in a similar way?

6. In the light of Billy Graham's comment (p. 102), discuss together what is involved in fulfilling your individual and joint responsibilities to this generation.

Afterword

So, despite my warning, you read the book! That was a big mistake, but all is not lost. I suppose you now believe that mission is very important indeed and that you must play your part in bringing the gospel to the world.

Well, that's fine, but let me give you a word of advice. This is far too important a matter to be rushed into without thinking. Why not put the book away for a few months and then see how you feel about things? There really isn't any hurry. Your tiny contribution is hardly going to change the world, so no one will worry if you delay making your contribution to world mission. You must think of your career, your financial security and your future plans—wouldn't it be better to get all these things sorted out before turning your attention to the ideas in this book?

And remember your image! No one likes a fanatic. Being too intense can be dangerous. Let's leave this passionate enthusiasm stuff for the athletic field or political rally. We don't want to put people off by our outspoken commitment to global evangelism—they might think we wanted to be as good as those early Christians the New Testament describes. Hell forbid!

So just relax and let the fuss die down. Your future is guaranteed; don't worry about the others. I'll take care of them for you. There is no need for you to bother—I will!

Lucy Fer

Resources

Key Books on Missions

Aldrich, Joe. *Life-Style Evangelism.* Sisters, Ore.: Multnomah Press, 1981.

Barnett, Betty. *Friend Raising: Building a Support Team That Lasts.* Seattle, Wash.: Youth With A Mission, 1991.

Beougher, Timothy. *Evangelism for a Changing World.* Wheaton, Ill.: Harold Shaw, 1995.

Borthwick, Paul. *A Mind for Missions.* Colorado Springs, Colo.: NavPress, 1989.

_____. *Six Dangerous Questions to Transform Your View of the World.* Downers Grove, Ill.: InterVarsity Press, 1996.

Duewel, Wesley. *Touch the World Through Prayer.* Grand Rapids, Mich.: Zondervan, 1986.

Gibson, Tim, et al., eds. *Stepping Out.* Seattle, Wash.: Youth With A Mission, 1992.

Griffiths, Michael. *Get Your Church Involved in Missions.* Littleton, Colo.: Overseas Missionary Fellowship, 1972.

Jansen, Frank Kaleb, ed. *Target Earth: The Necessity of Diversity in a Holistic Perspective on World Mission.* Kailua-Kona, Hawaii: Global Mapping International, 1989.

Johnstone, Patrick. *Operation World.* Grand Rapids, Mich.: Zondervan, 1993.

Myers, Glenn. *The World Christian Starter Kit.* Ft. Washington, Penn.: WEC, 1993.

Piper, John. *Let the Nations Be Glad.* Grand Rapids, Mich.: Baker Book House, 1994.

Pirolo, Neal. _Serving as Senders._ San Diego: Emmaus Road International, 1991.

Richardson, Don. _Eternity in Their Hearts._ Ventura, Calif.: Regal, 1984.

Stott, John. _Christian Mission in the Modern World._ Downers Grove, Ill.: InterVarsity Press, 1975.

Winter, Ralph, and Gerald Hawthorne, eds. _Perspectives on the World Christian Movement._ Pasadena, Calif.: William Carey Library, 1992.

Yamamori, Tetsunao. _Penetrating Missions' Final Frontier._ Downers Grove, Ill.: InterVarsity Press, 1993.

Mission Biographies

Crossman, Eileen. _Mountain Rain._ Littleton, Colo.: Overseas Missionary Fellowship, 1988.

Elliot, Elisabeth. _A Chance to Die: The Life of Amy Carmichael._ Grand Rapids, Mich.: Baker Book House, 1994.

_____. _Shadow of the Almighty._ Reprint ed. San Francisco: HarperSanFrancisco, 1989.

_____. _Through Gates of Splendour._ Reprint ed. Wheaton, Ill.: Tyndale House, 1988.

Kuhn, Isobel. _Green Leaf in Drought._ Littleton, Colo.: Overseas Missionary Fellowship, 1986.

_____. _Nests Above the Abyss._ Littleton, Colo.: Overseas Missionary Fellowship, 1988.

_____. _Stones of Fire._ Littleton, Colo.: Overseas Missionary Fellowship, 1989.

Magnusson, Sally. _The Flying Scotsman: Biography of Eric Liddell._ Boston: Charles River Books, 1982.

Muggeridge, Malcolm. _Something Beautiful for God._ San Francisco: HarperSanFrancisco, 1986.

Pullinger, Jackie. _Chasing the Dragon._ Ann Arbor, Mich.: Servant, 1980.

Sendall-King, Stuart. _Hope Has Wings: The Mission Aviation Fellowship Story._ Grand Rapids, Mich.: Zondervan, 1994.

Taylor, Mrs. Howard. _Pastor Hsi._ Littleton, Colo.: Overseas Missionary Fellowship, 1989.

Audiovisuals

Beyond the Church Walls. Available from InterVarsity Video, P.O. Box 7895, Madison, WI 53707-7895.

Concerts of Prayer. Available from Regal Books, 2300 Knoll Dr., Pasadena, CA 93003.

Cry Justice. Available from Regal Books, 2300 Knoll Dr., Pasadena, CA 93003.

Every Member Evangelism. Available from InterVarsity Video, P.O. Box 7895, Madison, WI 53707-7895.

Friends—Ministry Among International Students. Available from Inter-Varsity Video, P.O. Box 7895, Madison, WI 53707-7895.

God Is Building a City. Available from InterVarsity Video, P.O. Box 7895, Madison, WI 53707-7895.

God So Loved the World. Available from InterVarsity Video, P.O. Box 7895, Madison, WI 53707-7895.

To Every People. Available from InterVarsity Video, P.O. Box 7895, Madison, WI 53707-7895.

Prayer Resources: Periodicals
AD 2025 Global Monitor (newsletter)
GEM Research
1301 N. Hamilton, Suite 209
Richmond, VA 23230

Church Around the World (leaflet)
Tyndale House Publishers
P.O. Box 80
Wheaton, IL 60189

DAWN Report (magazine)
DAWN Ministries
7899 Lexington Dr., Suite 200B
Colorado Springs, CO 80920

Evangelical Missions Quarterly (journal)
Evangelical Missions Information Service
P.O. Box 794
Wheaton, IL 60189

FrontierScan (leaflet)
U.S. Center for World Mission
1605 Elizabeth St.
Pasadena, CA 91104

Global Prayer Digest (magazine)
U.S. Center for World Mission
1605 Elizabeth St.
Pasadena, CA 91104

International Journal of Frontier Missions (journal)
International Student Leaders Coalition for Frontier Missions
P.O. Box 27266
El Paso, TX 79926

Mission Frontiers (magazine)
U.S. Center for World Mission
1605 Elizabeth St.
Pasadena, CA 91104

Pulse (newsletter)
Evangelical Missions Information Service
P.O. Box 794
Wheaton, IL 60189

Prayer Resources: Internet
Advance
Contact Mark Kelly at 70420.1057@compuserve.com
Advance is a free monthly e-mail newsletter focused on prayer for
  unreached people groups and persecuted believers.

Brigada Today
http://www.xc.org/brigada/today
Brigada Today is a weekly bulletin, posted Friday mornings, with
  news and information about the Brigada "family" of mission net-
  works.

Current Trends & Updates
http://www.3rdworld.org/trends.html
At this website is a newsletter "ministering to servants of God in
  isolated places." It is a publication of the Third World Baptist
  Missions Network.

Global Evangelization Movement
http://www.goshen.net/gem

This website offers extensive material on unevangelized peoples. Global Evangelization Movement also offers two mailing lists: reality-check@xc.org, a weekly essay that deals with trends and events that affect the unevangelized peoples of the world, and gem-persecution@xc.org, a list of information on the persecuted church and specific instances of martyrdom.

The Lausanne Movement
hub@xc.org
The Lausanne Movement provides an e-mail conference on international Christian research issues and projects. To participate, send e-mail to the above address with "subscribe Lausanne-Research" in the body of the message. If you have any problems, contact helpdesk@xc.org.

The Missionwatch Report
hub@xc.org
This is a biweekly newsletter scanning the various countries of "World A," the unevangelized world (or the 10/40 Window), and listing special prayer items. To subscribe, send a message to the above address with the words "subscribe missionwatch" in the body of the message.

PrayerNet
brigada-us-prayertrack@xc.org
PrayerNet is a weekly e-mail newsletter published by the U.S. Prayer Track of the AD2000 & Beyond Movement and Mission America. It is designed to provide prayer intercessors with encouragement, inspiration and instruction.

Key Resource Groups in the U.S.A.
Association of Church Mission Committees
P.O. Box ACMC
Wheaton, IL 60189

Association of International Mission Services (AIMS; provides missions resources for charismatic churches)
P.O. Box 64534
Virginia Beach, VA 23464

Evangelical Fellowship of Mission Agencies (EFMA; brings together
   leaders of many different missions organizations)
1023 15th St. NW, Suite 500
Washington, DC 20005

Harvest International (for help in twinning with a church
   overseas)
1979 E. Broadway #2
Tempe, AZ 85282

Helps International Ministries
http://www.xc.org/helpintl/mrd.htm
This is an extensive mission "directory of directories" that enables you
   to link to the website of almost any missions organization.

Martin International (a travel agency that can help you plan a
   short-term missions trip)
8219 Denver St.
Ventura, CA 93004

Missions Advanced Research and Communications Center (MARC)
919 W. Huntington Dr.
Monrovia, CA 91016

SCUPE (provides training in urban missions)
30 W. Chicago Ave.
Chicago, IL 60610

Resource Groups/Persons in Other Countries
European Evangelical Alliance
Postfach 23
A-1037 Wien, Austria

Arbeitsgemeinschaft Evangelikaler Missionen (AEM)
Hindenburgstrasse 36
7015 Korntal-Munchingen 1, Germany

COMIBAM International
Apdo. Postal 27-1, CP 1907
Guatemala

India Missions Association
Post Box 2529
Madras 600 030, India

Vishal Mangalwadi
105 Savatri Commercial Complex
Greater Kailash II
New Delhi 110048, India

Association of Evangelicals of Africa and Madagascar
P.O. Box 49332
Nairobi, Kenya

Evangelische Alliantie (EZA)
Hoofdstraat 51-A
3971 KB Driebergen-Rijsenburg, Netherlands

Evangelical Missionary Alliance
P.O. Box 68-140
Auckland 1032, New Zealand

Pedro Araña, Misión Urbana y Rural
Apartado 21-0005
Lima 21, Peru

Singapore Centre for Evangelism and Missions
116 Lavendar Street
#04-07 Pek Chuan Building
Singapore 1233

Caesar Molebatsi, Youth Alive Ministries
P.O. Box 129
Soweto, Republic of South Africa

Ajith Fernando, Youth for Christ
P.O. Box 1311
Colombo, Sri Lanka

Notes for Group Leaders

Chapter 1: Becoming a World Christian

1. If your group is geographically based (if all members live in the same neighborhood or city), set them the task of finding out as much as they can about the locality. Use a future meeting to put the information together, and then make it a basis of prayer and action. You can do the same for any part of the world.

2. Use the ideas on page 16 to compose a group letter to a missionary known to the group. Pass out pens and paper and give members time to make their contributions. Or you might make a cassette tape or even a video instead of a letter.

Chapter 2: The Ultimate Authority

1. Open up the discussion by allowing several people to contribute their answers before focusing in on any particular point. Record the answers, then choose from them to focus and develop the issues.

2. Always try to ask open questions (ones that allow more than one answer). Then let more than one answer be offered.

Chapter 3: What Is a Missionary?

1. Encourage members of your group to tell their stories. Get the group to draw out the principles of telling, demonstrating and encountering from these stories. Aim to show how involvement in these actions is within reach of everyone in the group.

2. Keep the discussion moving by asking different group members to build on others' ideas. This also keeps members listening to each other.

Chapter 4: Who Will Go?

1. Begin your discussion by dividing the group into threes and asking them to draw up a list of basic qualifications for missionary service. Put the answers on a master list. Put a *C* beside those that relate to the quality of a person's character. Compare your list to Hudson Taylor's on page 57.

2. Perhaps someone in your group senses that God is nudging them to go. If so, pause and have the group pray with them about this. You may want to have a time in quiet to allow people to reflect on their own willingness to go.

3. New or quieter members of the group can be encouraged to participate by reading out the Scripture passages listed with the discussion questions. If they are new to the Bible, point out the passage before the discussion starts.

Chapter 5: Ready to Go?

1. Have each member state his or her area, then explore as a group what to do to help them develop. Don't forget to share yourself—you are part of the group.

2. Try to pursue people's answers by giving specific feedback or asking a follow-up question. For example, if "listening to people" is mentioned as a skill, ask something like "How do I know if you are listening to me?"

3. Always receive people's contributions positively, even if you disagree with them. A simple "Good" or "Thank you for that" doesn't cost much, but goes a long way to encourage more contributions.

Chapter 6: A Mission-Minded Church

1. To prevent this session from becoming overly critical, concentrate on issues within the sphere of influence of your group. Put together a suggestions sheet that you can pass on to your church leaders.

2. Try having a brainstorming session to generate ideas for creative contact support of a missionary known to your group (p. 84). Remember, in brainstorming all contributions are accepted and recorded, no

matter how offbeat or unworkable. No judgments are made. The purpose is to get the group's creative juices flowing.

Chapter 7: Heroes for a World in Need

1. Spend some time considering unbelievers known to you and your group. Use the account of Edward Kimball to stimulate imaginative prayer for the influence of members on the world through their relationships with these unbelievers.

2. Try to vary the style and interaction in group times. Take some time in pairs or threes as well as time all together.

The leader's notes and discussion questions in this book were prepared by Phil Cuthbert.